I0149999

Think For Real

Edwin J. Dunbar Jr.

Think For Real

Copyright © 2015 by Edwin J. Dunbar Jr.

All rights reserved. No part of this book may be reproduced or transmitted in any form or by any means without written permission of the author.

ISBN 9780986405556

Preface

This book was written out of a need to follow instructions when it is given by the Holy Spirit of God. I always wanted to write a book. But I had a very big problem with myself, letting self-get in the way. Always telling myself that I was not a writer. Several years ago while reading and studying my scriptures in my bible, mining my own business, learning to be a good Christian, the Holy Spirit of God placed in my mind to write a book; 12/20/2000 @ 10:00 pm. I thought I was just tired of reading because I had been reading for a while so I took a short break. After my break I switched books and began to read an interesting book I had purchased. While reading this book, the Holy Spirit of God placed in my mind for the second time to write my first book of many to come. I ignored it and put it in the back of my mind because I am not a writer as I had said to myself so many times. Around 11:39 pm I took another short break from reading because I had been reading for the last four hours, since 7:00 pm that night. While on my break I heard that same small voice reminding me to write the book so I said Okay Lord I will get right to it and start making my notes on the computer but I have no idea of what to write about and who is going to read it. (That's my thinking at that time). But the Lord knowing my future said different from my thinking. The next day I woke up and in the morning, I got on my computer and opened a new folder "title book writing". I felt real good that I kept my word and was now ready to start doing something. After that morning, somewhere along the way I forgot to do what I had Okayed to the Lord. On 11/20/14 while looking in my bible for some scriptures I came across this note between the pages with the date of 12/20/2000 written on it so I decides to take a look to find out what was on it. It read: I promise to write the book and to start right away. I said Lord forgive me. How did all this time get past me? I felt real bad for not obeying the Lord plus I still had no title or idea of what to write about. I asked myself, where do I start? The only words that came out of my mouth were forgive me Lord and I thank you Holy Spirit of God for not giving up on me in Jesus Name. Your man of God, Edwin J. Dunbar Jr., as of 11/20/14 I will truly write for real. Completion date? But to all of you who read this book and put into effect the simple truths, my sincere thanks to you with a grateful heart because you have caught the vision of THINK FOR REAL by keeping things simple of what Jesus is saying to the body of Christ today as the Holy Spirit of God help us live the Christian life style. Note: That this book is not a book of proven science, but suggestions of why and how to define and minister to problems that are physical, mental, and spiritual. Because of the lack of using our common sense, the Holy Spirit Of God still want us to overcome and gain success in whatever we are faced with. Use him and be blessed.

Introduction

ALERT .... ALERT .... ALERT

Read this page at your own risk

This book is not designed for everyone. However, everyone can find some important information here for his or her use. This book is designed specifically for those who have a desire, a want, how to do or a need for themselves or for someone they know, like, love, or care about. You can take what's on these pages and rearrange them to fit your life style. This information is also design to keep you from memorizing it and to show you why it is necessary to understand it. It will work on your behavior as you take the information here and rearrange it to fit your life style. Whatever it is that is standing between you or those you like, love, or care about, you will find it here as you rearrange things to fit your life style or help them with theirs. The chapters here in are self-help, how to do, and are not set in any specific order to flow from one chapter to the other. This is done to assist the readers in working on their patience in gaining only what applies to you and understanding how to rearrange it to fit your life style. You have nothing to lose and everything to gain as you control your patience for a short period of time to get what you want or need from these pages. You can do it if you try.

You say: I really don't want to change right now. But I know someday I need to or should change. I want to change or I might change if I feel like it. Or after I get rid of what I am faced with right now. I don't change now because I can't. But it's good to know what's in here on these pages in case I need it someday.

Over all we make attempts to change. Because of excuses and many other reasons, some failures happens along the way but those who said I am going to take another try at this, gained success because they refused to give up and they had patience to control their behavior. They made a choice to give this one more try. Especially those who have been beat down and beat up by varies religions. So what's the big deal? Take The Risk. You've got nothing to lose and everything to gain as you put to use what you rearrange to fit your life style.

If you have read this far; You've Done Well, the risk is now behind you. You've got nothing to lose. The rest is easy for you to gain your share of success which comes in varies forms. The best is still yet to come into your path, your life, and your way of living to gain your share of all successes that awaits you. Stay smart and collect.

Table of Contents

1. Defining Some Key Words

Let us start off by defining the words thinking and real.

Thinking

Thinking .... Using thought or rational judgment, intelligent, also the process of using one's mind to consider or reason about something.

Real

Real .... Actually existing as a thing or occurring in fact, not imagined or supposed. Also of a substance or thing, not imitation or artificial; (Is Genuine).

So we now see that it is possible to think for real. Our life and our family safety and success depend on thinking for real. Our health, our wellbeing, our success and our prosperity depends on us thinking for real. Maintaining our healing depends upon our thinking for real. Now let's look at a few more words.

2. Let's Start With: Fun

Fun ……….   Someone or something that's amusing or enjoyable experience or person. Also an enjoyable or amusing time. The feeling of being amused. Positive fun requires thinking for real. Serving Jesus, God, and The Holy Spirit of God is fun as we think for real.

Devil ………. Enemy of God and man kind. The personification of evil. We have power over the devil and his angels if we have the power of the Holy Spirit of God within us and know how to use His power. We must think for real in order to overcome with the Holy Spirit of God.

Holy Spirit of God ………. The One that Jesus sent back to earth to guide and direct us in all truths. The One who does everything for us. God added to that by saying: "Complete everything in the Name of Jesus "after the Holy Spirit of God has done His part and the Word of God will not return to God or us undone. Ephesians 4:30 ………." And do not grieve the Holy Spirit of God". The Holy Spirit of God power used on your behalf, completed by saying in the Name of Jesus, is a win; win for any one, anytime. The Holy Spirit is not an impersonal force. He is active in our lives, a distinct person, and fully God.

THINK FOR REAL ……………….

3. The Holy Spirit Job - in Part - Keeping Things Simple

Remember to keep things simple because the Holy Spirit does all the big, hard, and difficult things for us and leave the simple parts for us to do. His job is; to live inside of us, and monitor the earth. Teach us all truths and give us all secret and hidden riches that are ours. Monitor the earth and assist us with everything big or small. He dispatches our angels that were created for us to keep charge of us. Each and every one of us has an angel that was created and assigned to us for our use. They work for us as the Holy Spirit of God instructs them and dispatches them on our behalf. He gives them the command to work for us.

Check Point # 1 ………………..
You cannot use what you don't know of. We do our part and the Holy Spirit does His part. We than complete it in the Name of Jesus for it to work by simply saying; "In the Name of Jesus."

THINK FOR REAL ………………

THANK YOU JESUS. THANK YOU HOLY SPIRIT OF GOD. THANK YOU GOD OR THANK YOU FATHER GOD. WHY IS THANK YOU SO IMPORTANT IN THE THINGS OF GOD? (Thanks for asking).

Thank you is saying from you, I believe it before I physically see my results. Thank you Jesus is faith in action. This is what makes God move on your behalf. Telling God I believe it is done in my favor before you know the outcome. One key element in your car engine that makes your car move on your behalf is gas, so it is with thank you in the things of God that makes Him move on your behalf. If you want God to move on your behalf, never leave out thank you Lord or thank you Father God, or thank you Jesus, or thank you Holy Spirit of God in Jesus Name.

THINK FOR REAL ....

4. Trinity

Trinity .... God THE FATHER, GOD THE SON, AND GOD THE HOLY SPIRIT. We cannot separate them. They are the only ones who can separate themselves. Whatever way or however they tell us to use them, it is always in our best interest to do so. They have made everything simple for us to use and follow. They have done the hard and difficult parts for us and our parts are simple. So always keep it simple. If you find things hard and difficult, check to make sure it is from God before you do anything with it.

THINK FOR REAL ....

God .... The Supreme Being and Principal Object of Faith. The creator of everything. The only capital G – God there is. The real God. (Genuine).

5. Jesus

Jesus .... The son of God. He is also God. He also was the Word of God and still is. He has many functions. He died on the cross for mankind and rose from death to go to His Father in Heaven where He continues His work for mankind. Never look for Him on the cross. You serve a God that is bigger than that. He did what He had to do to free and save mankind. He cannot do anything for you if He has to stay on the cross. At this point what is important to you? Wasting time on why He did what He did or moving forward on what He wants us to do today in our life time here on the earth. He will be back someday and will like to see we have moved forward positively in the work He left for us to do. Jesus Christ is the central figure of Christianity. He paid the price for our sins. He wants us to not spend time on anything that will keep us from moving forward with what He has commanded us to do. How many of us ever worry about why our engines in our cars work? Why is it working to take us to where we want to go? How was it made and what was used to make them? How will that help us before we get in it and drive off? No one cares about that. We want to put gas in if we are low on gas and get to our appointment for the day. If you have one of these cars that needs charging, you will want to make sure it is charged and ready to take you to your destination. So it is with Jesus, He's not competing with anyone. He does not want us wasting our time on things concerning Him that we can do nothing about. He has instructed us to move forward in the things of God before His return. It is in our best interest to follow his instructions. It's one thing to listen to stories about Jesus, but it is a blessing to know Jesus and follow His commands for our lives. Never get caught up in the moment of storytelling about Jesus Christ. It is best to know your Jesus and follow His commands for your life and take charge of your successful future. You can't go wrong if you know Jesus for yourself. Let's look at some more words. We will start with bad.

THINK FOR REAL ………………..

6. Bad

Bad ………….. Not good in any manner or degree. Also as (wicked, evil, depraved). The enemy of God and mankind is evil and bad. The devil is bad and evil. There is nothing good about him. He is a liar. He tells every individual the same lies. He hates the truth. No one can tell us or show us anything that the devil have created or made from the beginning of time till now. He dislikes what God likes and causes trouble for those who like what God likes. The devil tries to make people believe in a friendly way that bad is good. (Ex: that music, that boxer, that football team, or that performer, just to name a few is bad in a friendly way for saying good). He does not like the word good by getting right to the point. Most people view this as harmless. Not understanding that this is a part of the devil plan in a small and friendly way of changing and reprograming your mind little by little. Because people can't see him, feel him, smell him, hear him, or touch him they have no idea what to look out for. In our example people think it sounds good and means good, and it's really no big deal. From the beginning of mankind bad have always been defined as bad and not good and no matter how you think it out, it will always remain defined as bad, not good. Continue to think for real.

7. Good

Good .... Favorable, acceptable, satisfactory, commendable, well – behaved, kind beneficent, honorable or worthy, virtuous, desirable, salutary, pleasant, valid, efficient, suitable, considerable, sufficiently. God is good and will always be good. It is good, favorable and acceptable to believe in God, trust in God, and follow His commands at all times. God showed His goodness by creating mankind. The devil has never created anything in his lifetime and will never be able to because he is bad and no good is found in him and his deeds. Being good as a devil is not part of his job on the earth.

8. Lie

Lie .... A false statement, an intentionally false statement to a person or group made by another person or group who knows it is not wholly the truth. Prevarication, falsification, a false statement made with deliberate intent to deceive, an intentional untruth. The devil job is to lie. He cannot tell the truth because that is not part of his job description. It does him no good to tell any truth. He tells the same lies to every individual he comes across or in contact with. Lie is worth more than gold to the devil. He can't help it. That's who he is and what he does daily. It is a way of life for him.

True .... Consistent with fact or reality; not false or erroneous. Real, genuine, being in accordance with the actual state or conditions, conforming to reality or fact; not false. God is true. He can't help it, that's part of His nature.

THINK FOR REAL ....

9. Wrong

Wrong .... Not in conformity with fact or truth, not correct in action, judgment, opinion, incorrect or erroneous, method not proper or usual, not in accordance with right, immoral or wicked, unfair, unjust, contrary or conscience. It is an act that is illegal or immoral. Anything or act that is not right is wrong no matter how you try to polish it or justify it.

Right .... Morally or socially correct or acceptable, agreeing with the facts or truth, accurate or correct, that which is morally correct or honorable, morally good, justifiable or acceptable, true or correct as a fact, correctly; speaking, acting, or judging in a way that agrees with the facts, or in conformity with fact, reason, truth, or some standard of principle, correct, the right solution, the right answer, correct in judgment, opinion or action. Anything or act that is the opposite of wrong is right.

10. False

False .... Contrary to fact or truth, in consistent impressions, ideas, or facts used as a substitute or supplement, deception in the form of an untruthful statement, not real or genuine, not true or accurate, especially temporarily, deliberately untrue, done or said to fool or deceive someone. False, does not line up with truth. Not according to truth or fact, in correct, appearing to be what is not actually so the thing denoted, deliberately made or meant to deceive. The devil deeds are all false made to appear truthful. Beware of his traps. Remember that's his job, he can't help it. Plus, using people.

Truth .... The real facts about something, the things that are true, the quality or state of being true, a statement or idea that is true or accepted as true. Truth is most often used to mean being with fact or reality, or fidelity to an original or to a standard or idea. The true or actual state of a matter, a verified or indisputable fact, conformity with fact or reality. God and everything about Him is truth as they line up with the Word of God. He tells us that we are more than our body, our mind, our personality, and our egos. We are a great soul with access to these hidden truths whenever we need them. That's The Holy Spirit of God job to see to it that we receive. We must do our part to allow Him to do His part for us. You must not let yourselves be distressed. You must hold on to your faith in God, The Holy Spirit of God, and Jesus. You can't go wrong with these three truths.

11. Easy

Easy .... Not hard or difficult; requiring no great labor or effort. Capable of being accomplished or acquired with ease; posing no difficulty, free from pain, discomfort, worry or care, requiring or exhibiting little effort or endeavor. Jesus died for our sins. He rose from the dead and gives us The Holy Spirit of God with power to make everything easy for us. The Holy Spirit of God does all the difficult and hard task leaving us with the easy elementary task. Acquire this power today and start enjoying success in your near future.

Complicated .... To make something more difficult or confusing by causing it to be more complex. Consisting of many or composed of elaborately interconnected parts; complex, elements, intricate, involving complications, or complicated apparatus for measuring brain functions. People wondered why life has to be so hard and complicated for them. Why did God put this on us? Is He trying to teach us a lesson for the wrong things we've done? Note that it is not part of God job description to do such. Even in some cases where He ordered such to take place, the devil was the one who carried it out. That's part of the devil's job.

12. Check Point # 2

Check Point # 2 ....
The devil job in part is to make things for us difficult or confusing by causing it to be more complex. He knows that you don't know that Jesus has made all things easy for you and He tells you that if it is not difficult or complex than it must not be from God. The truth of the matter is: if you find any parts that are complicated, double check to make sure that it is from God. The devil cannot defeat God but he can defeat the people of God for their lack of knowledge and their lack of the Holy Spirit of God power.

THINK FOR REAL ....

13. Spiritual

Spiritual .... Of or pertaining to the spirit or soul, as distinguished from the physical nature, relating to a person's spirit, a process of personal transformation in accordance with religious ideas. Relating to religion or religious beliefs, having similar values, spiritual but not religious, spiritual approach to life, Spirituality means something different to everyone. For some, it's about participating in organized religion; going to church, synagogue, a mosque, philosophy, meditation, and mainstream religion, nutrition, wellness, closely akin in interests, attitude, outlook, etc. The bottom line is: don't be so spiritual and no earthly good. How do you expect God to use you for His work here on earth? Don't become so spiritual that you fail to hear the voice of the Lord reaching out to you. If your spirituality becomes complicated, make sure it is from God and not self or the devil. Any spiritual practice that God is not a part of is; of self or the devil. Like it or not. That's what it comes down to.

14. Faith

Faith .... Belief that does not rest on logical proof or material evidence. Hebrews 11:1 (NEB)

Faith........makes us certain of realities we do not see. Faith, Hebrews 11:1 (MOD) means that we are confident of what we hope for. Faith is belief that is not based on proof. It can also be defined as confidence or trust in a person, thing, deity, view, or in the doctrines or teachings of a religion. The most important of all is faith in your Creator. Everything else is secondary. Put only your trust, hope, & faith in God for a positive result in any area of concern. Confident belief in the truth, value, and trustworthiness of your Creator. The only living God in heaven and on Earth. The devil is the small g-god of this world.

15. Religious

Religious................. Believing in a god or a group of gods and following the rules of a religion. Very careful to do something whenever it can or should be; Having or showing belief in and reverence for God or a deity, of concerned with, or teaching relating to or believing in a religion. Generally speaking, certain groups that don't acknowledge the existence of one or more deities. An organized collection of beliefs, cultural systems, and world views that relate humanity to an order of existence. Though we can't prove the existence of one (or many) god(s), we can provide evidence for the rules of religion. Remember that when God put the devil and his angels out of heaven He did not take away the power from the devil. So we have the power of the devil and the power of God on the earth. Choose the power of God. You can't go wrong. God is not religious; He is the only true God.

THINK FOR REAL................

16. Women of God

Women of God................ A woman after God's own heart and deeply sensitive to the spiritual things of God for His people. She is a believer in God and has a desire to read God's Word and grow in her faith. Genesis 2:18................ Then the Lord God, said, it is not good for the man to be alone; I will make him a helper suitable for him. For this is how the holy women who hoped in God used to adorn themselves, by submitting to their own husbands, as Sarah obeyed Abraham, calling him Lord. God is calling women to various roles in ministry today. As these women seek the Lord, He is opening doors for them. While each woman may have a unique gift, your labor is not in vain.

17. Man of God

Man of God................ Is the description given to a man (not a religious man). A man that follows God in every way, who obeys His commands with joy, who does not live for things of this world. But are given things from this world to further the Word of God to people everywhere possible. When you are a man of God who is after God's own heart, you are deeply sensitive to spiritual things. The calling to serve God is a calling to a position of special honor. Paul designates Timothy, (and equally all faithful ministers) and men and women of God in today's world to respect and apply the teachings of Jesus to everyone as they hold the title of "men of God or women of God". Standing firm in today's world as a solid, sold out man of God may seem like an impossible calling that's only a fit for prophets and preachers. But the call to true service is for every believer in God who takes action on His word. We must do our part and God will do His part. Each individual is challenged to get into God's Word to serve others and to grow up in the faith. 1 Timothy 6:11, "But you, Timothy are a man of God; so run from all evil things."(Run means do not part take). Pursue righteousness, steadfast, and a godly life, along with faith, love, perseverance and gentleness.

Check point # 3 .... It is best to be a man of God or a woman of God (God with a capital (G)) and not a man or woman of god with a small (g). Stay smart.

THINK FOR REAL ....

18. Business

Business .... Also known as an enterprise or a firm, it is an organization involved in the trade of goods, services, or both to customers. Doing God's business is a good way of allowing Him to work in and through you everywhere you go with signs and wonders following.

Play .... Is a range of voluntary, intrinsically motivated activities normally associated with recreational pleasure and enjoyment. A Christian life in part consist of, fun, play, enjoyment, claiming the promises of God, gaining a successful life style, voluntary submission to God and taking action on the Word of God to get what He's promise us. A Christian is strong and not weak. He or she has the power of the Holy spirit of God living on the inside of them. With such power and knowledge of how to use it, you have no time to be weak. You have enough power to defeat God's enemy. You also have enough power to live the Christian life style. And enough power to become successful.

19. Command

Command .... To direct with authority, give orders to, have control or authority over; rule, a general who commands, to give (someone) an order, to tell (someone) to do something in a forceful and often official way, to have authority and control over (a group of people), to deserve and receive, to have or exercise authority or control over, be master of, have at one's bidding or disposal. As Christians (meaning: Christ Like), who do we follow? We follow the One who give His life for us and died for our sins. Jesus. We are to do what Jesus did here on earth and even greater things. If Jesus prayed for something during His time here on earth we should do the same things during our time here on earth. If Jesus commanded certain things while He was here on earth we should also command certain things here on earth during our time. "NO EXCEPTIONS".

Check Point # 4 .... Jesus did not pray for everything while He was here on earth. He commanded some things. We as Christians living in today's world must do the same things if we are following Jesus. Have you ever thought about why some people fail to get their prayers or request granted or answered? I assure you there could be many reasons. However, if you should be praying for something and you are commanding it or if you should be commanding something and you are praying for that thing what kind of results would you be expecting? If you want positive results, pray where Jesus prayed and command where Jesus commanded. Use it in your life today within the time you have left here on the earth. Your job is not to make things happen or look for a certain feelings. Your job is to speak the word and take action on the word you have spoken. When you do your part, God will do His part. He never fails.

THINK FOR REAL ....

20. Speak

Speak .... To say words in order to express your thoughts, feelings, opinions, etc., to someone, to talk to someone, to talk about a particular subject or person. As Christians our job in part is to speak the Word of God. It is perfectly alright and okay to speak the Word of God. We might at times have to speak or try more than one method to get the job done. Do it boldly. Say what you want to take place. Speak it with authority, with your mouth. Hear your self-saying and speaking the Word of God with your mouth on any situation. Never try to get the job done by thinking it. Speak it, say it, and take action on the words you are speaking. Always make sure that what you speak or say line up with the Word of God.

Pray .... To speak to God especially in order to give thanks or to ask for something, to hope or wish very much for something to happen, to seriously ask for something from God, to offer devout petition, praise, thanks, etc. to God. The bottom line: when you pray you are calling on God for something or some reason. Asking God for something. Talking from you to God, from earth to heaven.

21. Check Point # 5

Check Point # 5 ……………….. Know when to pray to God. Know when you should be commanding. Also know when you should be calling things that are not as though they were. You have different results here so do the right thing to get the right results. Don't be praying when you should be commanding. Don't be commanding when you should be praying or calling things that are not as though they were. You will start to get more positive results as what you say or speak line up with the Word of God.

THINK FOR REAL ………………

22. Christian

Christian ……………….. Christ Like. Followers of Jesus Christ. Doing the same things Jesus did while He was on earth. He also charged us to do greater things because He is going to His Father in heaven and will still be working on our behalf.

Healing ……………… (Literally meaning to make whole) is the process of the restoration of health to an unbalanced, diseased or damaged organism. Faith healing is healing purportedly through spiritual means. To restore to health or soundness, cure. To restore (a person) to spiritual wholeness. To make healthy, whole, or sound, restore to health, free from ailment. To bring to an end or conclusion. To be completely and totally well as restoration of health is process in a person being made whole by the power of God.

Miracle ……………….. A miracle is an event not expli-cable by natural or scientific laws. An effect or extraordinary event in the physical world that surpasses all known human or natural powers and is ascribed to a Supernatural cause. The wonder of the miracle is due to the fact that its cause is hidden, and an effect is expected other than what actually takes place. A miracle or miracles are the supernatural things that God does for each individual who ask of Him. Miracles, signs and wonders are part of the benefits God have and give or cause His people to enjoy. It pays to be a part of the King-dom of God and what God wants to do for you today. You have nothing to lose by coming on board.

THINK FOR REAL …………………..

23. Prayer

Prayer .... Is an invocation or act that seeks to activate a rapport with a deity, an object of worship, or a spiritual entity through deliberate communication. Prayer is asking or thanking God for something. How do you know that your prayers are being heard by God? Are you allowing God to hear your prayers? Are you enjoying a break through to Him so He will hear and answer your prayers and requests? Well, let's check ourselves.

Check Point # 6 .... The Word of God tells us that if we hold anything against anyone while we pray God will not hear our prayers. Well let's start by saying; make sure you clear the gap before you start praying. If you want to enjoy a break through with your prayers to God than you must find ways to correct your entry into your prayers. You can try something like this; "Lord Jesus, I thank you for forgiving me for my sins as I forgive those that have sinned against me. I also thank you right now for this breakthrough to you as you hear and answer my prayer. I thank you for looking over your Word to perform it for me". The Word of God tells us that when we forgive those who have done anything against us God will also forgive us our sins. He will remember our sins no more, as far as the east is from the west. Now you have opened that gap so your prayers can be heard. It will be best if you practice this one on every prayer you want to pray to God. It takes nothing away from you or your prayers by doing this. But it leaves no room for error in the start of your prayers. We serve a God who really wants to hear from us. So don't disappoint Him by trying to get Him to go against His own Word. Do things right the first time around and expect God to answer you every time as He look over His Word to respond to you. He's ready and waiting for you. He can't wait to hear from you.

THINK FOR REAL ………………

24. Fasting

Fasting .... Is primarily an act of willing abstinence or reduction from certain or all food, drink, or both, for a period of time. Fasting is the most powerful spiritual discipline for all the Christian disciplines. Through fasting and prayer, The Holy Spirit of God can transform your life. An absolute fast is normally defined as: intermittent fast. Starvation response – juice fasting etc. Prayer and fasting also relates to abstaining from food for the purpose of focusing on God. As you rely on Him for wisdom and direction He will answer. Some people use fasting as a way to lose weight and cleanse the body of toxins. A person's entire immune system can be rejuvenated by fasting for as little as three days as it triggers the body to start producing new white blood cells counts. During extended fasts the body removes: dead, dying and diseased cells, unwanted fatty tissue, trans-fatty acids, hardened coating of mucus on the intestinal walls. Some believe the power of fasting as it relates to prayer is the spiritual atomic bomb that our Lord has given us to destroy the strongholds of evil among other things. Since the time of Adam, God's people have fasted to help them draw near to God and to worship Him. Jesus also showed the importance of fasting. It is also written, how can some things come out except by prayer and fasting. Make use of it for your future is still ahead of you.

25. Heal

Heal .... To become sound or healthy again. (Of a person or treatment) cause (a wound, injury, or person). To restore to health or soundness; cure. To make whole, free from ailment. To restore (a person) to spiritual wholeness. To set right, repair, healed the rift between us, to bring to an end or conclusion.

Check Point # 7 .... If you are suffering from a disease, an injury, or a chronic medical condition, you may wonder if you can ever be healed. The bible has good news for you. According to psalm 107:20 He (Jesus) sent His Word and healed them. He issued His command and healed them; He delivered them. As Christians we should be doing the same things Jesus did. We should speak our words or commands using our own mouth making sure it line up with the word of Jesus and send it as well. So what do we need in order to make this work? We need the power of the Holy Spirit of God and in the Name of Jesus to effectively send ours. So if you have not invited the Holy Spirit of God and Jesus to live in and through you, make sure you do so if you want to have access to this power. And straightway the fountain of her blood was dried up, and she felt in her body that she was healed of the plaque.

26. Example # 1

Example # 1 .... Let's take Psalm 107:20 we can say something like this: Lord Jesus, I thank you for forgiving me for my sins or wrong doings as I forgive those that have wronged me or sin against me. I also thank you for this breakthrough to you. Holy Spirit of God, I thank you for living inside of me and causing me to have favor with God and men in Jesus Name. Father, I thank you for looking over your word to perform it in my life daily. I thank you for giving me favor with God and with men as I call things that are not as thou they were, as I am calling and speaking things into existence. According to psalms 107:20 I send your word or I thank you for sending your word for the healing of __?____. At this point you say your part. (The reason for sending Ps. 107:20 on their behalf). Always remember that God is God and He can override what we do or say and do things completely different from what we are used to. Never fear, Let God have His way. It is His power, His word, and you belong to Him. This example is a little long but it's good for your practice. As you grow in the things of the Lord it will be a lot shorter and to the point.

27. Power

Power .... Power is the rate of doing work in physics. It is equivalent to an amount of energy consumed per unit time. In the MKS system, the unit of power is the joule. We have in existence to day; average power, mechanical power, electrical power, etc. In social science and politics, power is the ability to influence or control the behavior of people. The term authority is often used for power perceived as legitimate. Power is also the ability or right to control people or things; Political control of a country or area, a person or organization that has a lot of control and influence over others. There are so many different kinds and types of power; hydro power, nuclear, wind, and solar, gas and coal and etc. So let's compare all of these powers to the power of God, The Holy Spirit of God, and Jesus. God made those powers and made the people who work these powers. It will always be impossible for all the total sum of these powers to equal to the power of God. So think for real........ What power do you have living on the inside of you? If it is not the power of God, you need to adjust your thinking and except the power of God, working in and through you for a brighter future. Every other power you except inside of you will at some point and time destroy you but the greatest power of all (The true and living God) comes and dwells inside of you without destroying you in any manner. Think for real .... Only God can do that. You can't get any better than that.

28. Knowledge

Knowledge .... Facts, information, and skills acquired by a person through experience or education, the theoretical or practical understanding of a subject. Awareness or familiarity gained by experience of a fact or situation. Familiarity, awareness or understanding of someone or something, such as fact, information, descriptions, or skills, which is acquired through; tacit knowledge, knowledge management, intuition, self-knowledge, carnal knowledge, general knowledge, knowledge adventure, knowledge engineering, etc. Familiarity, awareness, or understanding gained through experience or study. The sum or range of what has been perceived, discovered, or learned. Acquaintance with facts, or principles, as from study or investigation; general erudition, knowledge of many things. Familiarity or conversance, general, human faculty resulting from interpreted information, understanding that germinates form combination of data, information, being a primitive fact of consciousness, cannot, strictly speaking, be defined, but the direct and spontaneous consciousness of knowing. Knowledge is power if you know how and when to apply it. Think for real what you have on the inside of you. What do you think your pastors and other likeminded individuals have been trying to get you to realize and understand? Medical knowledge, science knowledge and any other knowledge you can think of just stack them all against the knowledge of God and they all put together will never come close to the knowledge of God. And if you allow God to live inside of you with all that knowledge just think about how better of you will be as you learn to tap in it here and there and put it to use. That is knowledge you don't have to purchase. It comes with God as a package deal. The Holy Spirit of God will share that knowledge with you as you need it or request it but you must take action on it for it to work for you. You have the best package and best deal in the world. Collect your share now.

THINK FOR REAL ………………..

29. Bold

Bold ………………….. Not hesitating or fearful in the face of actual or possible danger or rebuff; courageous and daring, a bold hero, not hesitating to break the rules of propriety, requiring or exhibiting courage and bravery, unduly forward and brazen; impudent, clear and to the point. God want us to be bold. He doesn't want us to stop at being bold but to add some smarts to it. As Christians we understand that we serve a God who is alive, bold, brave, and smart. Knowing this we cannot afford to settle for less. If someone presents a weak Christian God to you, make sure you do your research on the matter. If you don't know how to do a research, ask other pastors or mature Christians on the matter. It will save your life if you put in the extra time to get answers.

30. Strong

Strong ………………….. Physical power; capable of exerting great physical force. Marked by great physical power, strong, powerful, mighty, able, firm, constant, resolute, strenuous, hardy, hard severe, fierce. Having the power to move heavy weights or perform other physically demanding tasks. Able to withstand great force or pressure. Having showing, or able to exert great bodily or muscular power, physically vigorous or robust: a strong boy. Accompanied or delivered by great physical force. Once again we point out that as Christians we serve a God that is strong and stronger than any force on earth. The Christian God is not stuck to the cross and He is not dead. He is ready, able and willing to strengthen you in every way and be a blessing to you.

31. Brave

Brave .... Ready to face and endure danger or pain; showing courage. Courageous, valiant, valorous, intrepid, and heroic, lion hearted, bold, fearless, gallant, daring, plucky, audacious people who are ready to face and endure danger or pain. Endure or face (unpleasant conditions of behavior) without showing fear. To face or endure with courage, possessing or exhibiting courage. To be able to look at your biggest fear and face it in the eye. To face certain dangers or situations, even though doing so is something that scares you. Remember that God does not give you the spirit of fear. That comes from the devil. Stay brave and ready. You have enough power on the inside of you to speak and take action on the Word of God and get positive results. If you are using the Holy Spirit of God power.

32. Strength

Strength .... The quality or state of being strong, in particular. A good or beneficial quality or attribute of a person or thing. The number of people comprising of a group, typically a team or army. The quality or degree of being strong. The quality or state of being physically strong. The ability to resist being moved or broken by a force. The quality that allows someone to deal with problems in a mental power force. The quality or state of being strong, bodily or muscular power, vigor, mental power, force, or moral power, firmness, or courage. The state, property, or quality of being strong. The power to resist attack, impregnability. The power to resist strain or stress; durability. The ability to hold your position and advance. As Christians we have all the strength we will ever need living inside of us which is The Holy Spirit of God. To use that strength, we have to renew our minds with the Word of God and speak His Word as we take action on those words we are speaking in the Name of Jesus. You can't go wrong. It's there for your use. You can't enjoy the positive results if you don't speak it and take action on what you are speaking. Keep it simple. It's easy if you speak it and take action on what you are speaking. It's not your job to make things happen. It's the Holy Spirit of God job in the Name of Jesus to make things happen.

33. Brain

Brain .... The brain is an organ that serves as the center of the nervous system in all vertebrate and most invertebrate animals—only a few invertebrates such as sponges etc. The human brain has been called the most complex object in the known universe, and in many ways it's the final frontier of science. A hundred billion neurons. You now see why the Holy Spirit of God takes care of all the complex things that concern us individually. If you are face with the complex things, that might take you away from serving God, make sure you double check the Word of God on whatever it is that you are faced with. Ten times out of ten it's the devil keeping you in a complex mode to draw you away from God. The exception to that statement is; if you know what you should do or be doing and you chose not to then your negative results rest on your own head. No one to blame but yourself.

34. Check Point # 8

Check point # 8 .... We know that when God got angry with the devil and his angels, and kicked them out of heaven they came down to earth. God did not take their powers away from them. (The devil without his powers is no devil at all). God allowed Jesus to come down to earth and take care of that problem. Now let's look at some important facts while keeping things simple and in our own words to get our point across. Let's start off like this: we have God the Father, the Holy Spirit of God, and Jesus, the Son of God, (who is also God – like it or not, He is). God made the heavens and the earth. He made everything there is including human beings. He made human beings in his own image and likeness. Our form is exactly the same as God. The devil saw this and he got real angry. He said I was here before these people came about so what makes God think He has the right to make people look like Him and not make me look like Him? He even gives them control over everything. I have to do something about that. The devil started causing trouble here and there and every opportunity he could come across with the people God had made. Now God went a little further and made man the controller of everything that God made. God then gave man a woman that He made just for the man. (Can you imagine being given a most beautiful woman just for you)? WOW!!! By this time the devil said okay I had enough of this one-sided treatment. I'm going to do something about it. He started talking to the man trying to get him to do what God said for him not to do. The devil was not getting good results with the man so he switched over to the woman and convinced her to do wrong against what God had said not to do. She then brought all that beauty and got in front of her husband and said will you like to try some of this that I am eating? The husband being the man he is said no, God said not to do that. She then said just look at me and he did ("I think this is where man failed because looking at such a most beautiful woman stopped his thinking for a moment. All he could see was the love of his life; God was not on his mind for that moment"). She said do you think I will do anything to hurt you? The devil is a friend she said. He even told me that God didn't really mean what he said and he has been with God from the beginning of everything that God have made so he knows how God thinks. God just didn't want us to be smarter than we already are. Or maybe think we will be smarter than God. (The man looked at his most beautiful wife and said "God, have mercy on me but this woman is my life, I can't see anything right now because this beauty got me in a bind and speechless"). After looking at her and listening to her, he gave in and did what God said not to do. Right after that God called him and he found himself trying to hide from God. Things had changed from the way God wanted things to stay for him and his wife. God asked the man, what have you done? He said God, the woman you give me hit me so hard with that beauty, I just couldn't think and before I knew it she had gotten me in trouble with you. God said that's no excuse. You, your wife, and the devil will pay the price for what you all have done. Then God kicked the devil out of heaven and down to the earth he came along with his angels. God also kicked man and his wife out of the garden. God charged the man and his wife with a guilty verdict and sentence them with the price they will have to pay for the rest of their lives. The devil was now on the earth with man but God did not take away his powers from him. Man could no longer physically see the devil, he remained stronger than man. So one day God, the Holy Spirit of God, and Jesus was talking and having some family time and Jesus said Father I need to point out something to you if it is okay with you and God said tell me what's on your heart. Jesus said Father, we made man in our own image and likeness for our enjoyment but you are too strong for them. If they come before you and are guilty, they die right away. People even had to tie a rope around their priest to be able to pull his body out from behind the prayer area if he didn't make it to come out alive. Father these people belong to me also. Please let me go down to earth and make things right. God said, "If you want to, I'm not going to stop you but you are doing so at your own risk." Are you willing to pay such a price for them? Jesus said yes I am willing. Jesus said I know that the devil doesn't like them because he doesn't like anything that we have made and he is constantly destroying our people and turning them against us. I have to go down and take care of this because they belong to us. How will they learn if I don't teach them and show them the way to overcome the devil and his tricks? So God knowing the beginning to the end said okay we will make the necessary arrangements for you to go down and take action on what you are going to earth to do. The keys to life were taken from man by the devil spiritually. So to give that back to man Jesus had to come and take it back from the devil spiritually. Keep in mind that spiritual things works differently from physical things. Jesus came down to earth and did what he had to do and took everything back that the devil had taken from man. Man had an idea that he had done wrong to God and by God standards, but he had no idea of the major damage he had caused spiritually. Even in today's world man still doesn't get it because man is trying to make the spiritual things physical. Now whatever you do spiritually God can allow you to enjoy the results physically but it is never your job to change that around because it will not work your way. Jesus said after completing his task here on earth that I've gotten everything back for you, I've trained you, and I've showed you the way, I now give back to you everything that was taken from you. Use it and enjoy it. Do what I've taught you. I am sending back to you the Holy Spirit of God who will assist you in everything. He will teach you all truths, renew your minds and monitor the earth. He will live in you and show you secrete hidden riches. He will help you do greater things than when I was here on earth. Do not grieve Him. He is on your side. Receive him because he has all the power you will ever need to get things done. So God stepped in and said I agree with what Jesus said to you but everything must be completed in the Name of Jesus if you want the positive results and the blessings that come with it. (So – by the power of the Holy Spirit of God in the Name of Jesus). God, The Holy Spirit of God, and Jesus are all one. They are the only ones who can divide themselves into three persons. This is one way or reason how you know they are really God. So don't be surprise if you only say in the Name of Jesus and things happen for you. They can choose to respond to your request any way they want. (If you have God, you also have the Holy Spirit of God, and Jesus. If you have the Holy Spirit of God, you also have God and Jesus. If you have Jesus, you also have the Holy Spirit of God and God the Father). It is always up to you to learn how each one wants to be accepted and used in your life as you follow their instructions and be blessed, or grieve one or the other or reject them and not be blessed. They will never force you to do anything. If you owe your bank for loans, they are going to come after you to collect but with Jesus who have paid the price for you and own you and your life, he is not going to come after you like your bank will to collect but by you rejecting him you will push yourself into hell. It's like the rule of gravity which states that what goes up must come down but it depends on you how you go up and how you come down to ensures that you are still alive when you are done. Don't push yourself into hell. Get help while you are still alive. Keep it simple. It is all real.

THINK FOR REAL ………………..

35. Weak

Weak .... Lacking the power to perform physically demanding tasks, lacking physical strength and energy. Liable to break or give way under pressure; easily damaged. Lacking intensity or brightness. Contrasted with strong. Having little physical power or ability, not strong, having little power or force, likely to break or stop working properly, not able to handle weight, pressure, of, redacting to, or denoting the weakest of the known kinds of force between particles, which acts only at distances less than about 10~ 15 cm, is very much weaker than electromagnetic and the strong interactions, and conserves neither strangeness, parity, nor isospin. Likely to fail under pressure, stress, or strain, lacking resistance, a weak link in a chain, lacking firmness of character or strength of will, lacking the proper will power. Not strong, liable to yield, break, or collapse under pressure or strain, fragile, frail, a weak fortress, a weak spot in armor. Lacking in bodily strength or healthy. In particle physics, the weak interaction is the mechanism responsible for the weak force or weak nuclear force, one of the four fundamental interactions of nature. You may feel weak but have no real loss of strength. This is called subjective weakness. It may be due to an infection such as mononucleosis or the flu. If you claim to be weak, let the Lord be your strength. Renew your mind with His word and take action on what you read and stay strong with the strength of the Lord. Use his power to cast out any infection or diseases that are keeping you weak. He has more than enough strength and power to share with every individual.

36. Smart

Smart .... High performance; top achievement, advanced memory or reasoning, goals that are specific, measurable, attainable, realistic and timely. Having or showing a quick witted intelligence. Clever, bright, intelligent, sharp – witted, quick – witted, shrewd, astute, able well dressed, stylish, chic, fashionable modish, elegant, neat, spruce, trim, dapper, intelligence, acumen, in a quick or brisk manner, Characterized by sharp quick thought, bright, amusingly clever. Having a clean, tidy, and stylish appearance. Renewing your mind daily with the word of God and taking action on the word you read will keep you smart and help you make more positive choices in every given day of the year. Stay smart, look smart, be smart, act smart, dress smart and live smart. Your future is still ahead of you. The best is still yet to come into your life. Your own successful lifestyle is waiting for you to take charge of it.

37. Mind

Mind .... In the set of cognitive faculties that enables consciousness, perception, thinking, judgment, and memory – a characteristic of humans. The part of a person that thinks, reasons, feels, and remembers, - used to describe the way a person thinks or the intelligence of a person. A very intelligent cognitive faculties (in a human or other conscious being) the element, part, substance, or process that reasons, thinks, feels, wills, perceives, judges, etc. Note that the truth comes from your heart. The mind and brain is where all the scratch work, confusion, and other problems are pushed around searching and or planning for a solution. The mind is where the devil attacks people in order to have his way with them. Then he attacks their body hopping to destroy it. Now be very careful at this point, just because you can't feel him, touch him, smell him, hear him, or see him doesn't mean he is not there with you. Remember that God did not take his powers away from him when he was kicked out of heaven down to the earth. Always trust the Holy Spirit of God to fill you in on the spiritual things and you wouldn't go wrong. You can only choose to go wrong and to do wrong. So if your mind is telling you something that does not line up with the word of God that you know and understand, and you are not sure about it because your heart doesn't feel good about what you are thinking, always read your bible to see what it says about the subject or matter at hand. Be smart and of good report. Your future is still ahead of you. The best is still yet to come in your life. The more positive choices you make in each given day, the more success you can expect and count on as a result of the actions you have taken. Keep your brain and your mind healthy.

38. Heart

Heart .... The heart is a muscular organ in humans and other animals, which pumps blood through the blood vessels of the circulatory system. The blood provides the necessary functions your heart and your entire body needs to stay alive. Your heart needs to stay clean and pure. Do not put junk in your blood because it will get to your heart and then to the rest of your body. We as human beings are blessed while we are alive because our heart never sleeps or stop working. The sad thing is; the more junk of any kind we put into our hearts forces it to want to stop working for us. If your heart stops working for you or goes to sleep on you, your body will shut down. You will not be allowed to move any longer. Without help in that area, that will be the end of you as a human being or person we have gotten used to seeing. Be smart, do the right things to keep your heart alive until it is your time to depart from the earth. Let's take a look at what your bible says about your heart and some of the things your heart is used for or in general, good for. Remember to keep it simple.

Luke 16:15 ..... But God knows your hearts.

John 14:1 ..... Do not let your hearts be troubled.

Acts 15:9 ..... For He purified their hearts by faith.

Ephesians 3:17 ..... So that Christ may dwell in your hearts through faith.

Hebrew 10:16 I will put my laws in their hearts.

2Corinthians 4:6 ….. For God, who said, "Let light shine out of the darkness," made His light shine in our hearts to give us the light of the knowledge of the glory of God in the face of Christ.

Leviticus 19:17 …. Do not hate your brother in your heart.

Deuteronomy 6:5-9 …… Love the Lord your God with all your heart and with all your soul and with all your strength. These commandments that I give you today are to be upon your hearts. Impress them on your children. Talk about them when you sit at home and when you walk along the road, when you lie down and when you get up. Tie them as symbols on your hands and bind them on your foreheads. Write them on the doorframes of your houses and on your gates.

THINK FOR REAL ………………

39. Body

Body .... The human body is the entire structure of a human being and comprises a head, neck, trunk, (which includes the thorax and abdomen), arms and hands, legs, feet etc. The human body is very important to God. He made it in His own image and likeness. Human form looks like him. God loves what he made. He do not regret making our bodies look like His. But He has an enemy who is also our enemy because this enemy the devil doesn't like us because God made us like Himself. And every time we remind the devil about God, because we look like God but without the powers of God he is ready to attack our bodies. This is one of the reasons why Jesus came and put a stop to the devils attack against God's people. The bible tells us that the devil is the one who is going around the world doing things that are not pleasing to God. If it is not pleasing to God, it also is not pleasing to human beings. The devil is negative and his job is to steal, kill, destroy, and lie to the people of God among other things. Just because you can't see him, feel him, touch him, smell him, and many other ways don't mean he is not around you at all times and at work doing what he does best. So be smart and use the power Jesus has given you to defeat the devil and stop him in his tracks of wrong doings and attacks on people.

1 Corinthians 6:15 ..... Do you not know that your bodies are members of Christ himself?

Ephesians 5:28 – 30 ..... Husbands ought to love their wives as their own bodies. He who loves his wife loves himself. After all no one ever hated his own body, but he feeds and cares for it, just as Christ does the church ---- for we are members of his body.

Matthew 10:28 ..... Do not be afraid of those who can kill the body but cannot kill the soul. (Referring to the devil and people lead by the devil), rather, be afraid of the One who can destroy both the soul and body in hell. (Referring to God).

Your body is the temple of God. You must not do anything you feel like doing to it. Jesus already paid the price for your body. He has given us the Holy Spirit of God and all the powers that come with him for our use. But we have to know how to get a hold of this power and use it. So at this point let's take one example.

40. Example # 2

Example # 2 .... Let's take a case like Ebola. This disease that scared so many people and killed so many people in 2014. As Christians we know that this is the job of the devil because it is not part of the job of God. Let's say we know nothing about this disease. But we know we have the power of the Holy Spirit of God in us for our use. We will ask the doctor what is this disease called and what is it doing to the body. The doctor will tell us this is Ebola. This is how it is affecting the body and killing people. (Now don't forget that the Holy Spirit of God does all the complex things for us). Never be afraid to check with the doctor and follow his instructions because the power of God can stand under any test. The doctor might alert you to what else is left in the body that needs to be removed. Don't ever play doctor but use the power of God and check with your doctor for progress report and follow the doctor instructions.

1. We have Ebola on someone. (The EVD Virus)
2. We know it kills.
3. It spreads from one person to another.
4. It makes the body weak and can't hold any fluids in.
5. It drains your body of life.
6. It causes shortness of breath, chest pains, swellings, maculopoula rash, headaches, fever, sore throat, muscle pain, vomiting, and diarrhea, decrease function of the liver and kidneys, bleeds both internally and externally, low blood pressure and a high risk of death killing those infected with the disease. At this point we must note that so much more is taking place that we might never learn of. However, it is not our job to know everything. That is the job for the Holy Spirit of God. Jesus paid the price for us to not have any of these

diseases upon our bodies. So if Jesus already took these diseases with him on the cross where he left them there, is no reason why we should have to allow them back on us. So never feel bad to say, Jesus, you already took these diseases with you so no need for me to carry it. I send it right back to the cross where you left it and I thank you in your precious Name Jesus for destroying it and sending it to hell where it belongs. I thank you Holy Spirit of God for taking care of this in Jesus Name.

7. Ministering to what we know about this disease. Note: don't try to remember everything. Write it on a sheet of paper and take it with you. Open your eyes, read and speak the words with authority. This is the time to command, not pray. You can pray on your own time .Right now some one life depends on your commands. You may start like this:

A. In the Name of Jesus and by the power of the Holy Spirit of God, devil I bind you and

B. I cast out the spirit of Ebola – EVD, from this body.

C. You foul spirit of death come out right now in Jesus Name.

D. I command life to come back into this body in Jesus Name and by the power of the Holy Spirit of God right now.

E. I curse the seeds, roots, and cells of this EVD virus and command all of it to die and not to spread any further in Jesus Name and by the power of the Holy Spirit of God.

F. I rebuke any headaches and pain and command them to cease and come out right now in Jesus Name. (Stretch your hand close to the body without touching it or point in that direction).

G. Now, by the power of the Holy Spirit of God I command every affected area of Ebola cells in this body to continue to die, dry up, and come out now in Jesus Name.

H. I thank you right now Holy Spirit of God for a creative miracle of a brand new immune system and a brand new blood system to go in this body.

I. I command the bone marrow to produce pure healthy blood to function properly with the new systems.

J. I command healing to all organs and tissues affected and restoration of parts where necessary.

K. I command the digestive system to be healed and I rebuke every infection in that area.

L. I command the body's defensive "killer" cells to multiply and attack all Ebola EVD cells in this body. I command the electrical and chemical frequencies in every cell in the body to be in harmony and in balance and to digest all the bad or sick cells in Jesus Name. I thank you Holy Spirit of God for looking over your word according to Mark 11:23 to complete this healing in Jesus Name.

Brain you signal every area of the body to show proper function and operation of systems in this body. Thank you Jesus for this healing.

Note: You can say thank you Jesus for this healing or if the individual is able, he or she can say thank you Jesus for my healing. Never ever leave this out. This is faith in action. This is what makes God move on your behalf. You are telling Him that you believe he have healed you without you first seeing your results. Note that God will never let you get away with this act of faith in Him thereby showing you that yes I am your God and I will out do you and give you what you ask of me. Encourage the individual if possible to check with his or her doctor for results because the power of God can stand under any test. Keep in mind and understand that from the time you started speaking the word of God over this individual, the power of God was at work in this individual's body. Continue to thank the Holy Spirit of God in Jesus Name for answering your request and commands over this individual.

Also thank God for looking over his word to perform it on your behalf in Jesus Name.

THINK FOR REAL ………………………..

41. Human Body

Human Body …………………….. It is the entire structure of a human being and comprises of a head, neck, trunk (which includes the thorax and abdomen), arms and hands, legs and etc. In the human body you have a heart which is a muscular organ about the size of a closed fist that functions as the body's circulatory pump. It takes in deoxygenated blood through the veins and supplies the entire human body. The heart is the body's engine room, responsible for pumping life sustaining blood. The heart pumps oxygen – rich blood throughout your body and oxygen – poor blood to your lungs without ever stopping to rest. This is one way you know that it is all God's doing. Everything we know of in today's world shuts down for maintenance sometime during operation while a back – up unit kicks on. The human body is the temple of God. God made this body in his own image. Jesus paid the price for our body. Be smart, keep it simple, and think for real. You can't go wrong with God.

42. Honest

Honest .... Honorable in principles, intentions, and actions; upright and fair: an honest person. Showing uprightness and fairness, honest dealings, gained or obtained. Honesty refers to a facet of moral character and connotes positive and virtuous attributes such as integrity, truthfulness, and straightforwardness. By being honest, you are creating a healthy and sustainable future for you and those you care about. Also those who believe in you and what you stand for. Honest means good and truthful, not lying, stealing, or cheating, but showing or suggesting a good and truthful character. Not hiding the truth about someone or something, not being dishonest. It has been said in the past that honesty is the best policy. However, if you have done wrong of any kind that requires a price to be paid for your wrong doing, honesty will not excuse you or prevent you from paying such price. So a good rule to follow is: if you are honest or dishonest, you will still have a price to pay so why not stay honest and be blessed by the Lord for the price you have to pay?

43. Practice

Practice .... Repeated performance or systematic exercise for the purpose of acquiring skill or proficiency, to do or perform habitually or customarily, make a habit of, the act of rehearsing a behavior over and over, or engaging in an activity again and again, for the purpose of improving or mastering it. To do something again and again in order to become better at it, to do (something) regularly or constantly as an ordinary part of life. To live according to the principles and practices of living a Christian life style also needs practice. Have you heard this old saying that states; practice makes perfect? I submit to you that regular practice or making practice a part of your life style will aid you in your success of positive results daily. It helps you to be sure of yourself in whatever you are doing.

44. Prayer Language

Prayer Language .... Most likely is a private prayer language that is not interpreted to anyone while praying in the spirit. Whereas praying in tongues needs an interpretation. The conclusion reached is that tongues are not earthly languages but a "heavenly" or special prayer language that in most cases need to be interpreted because God is giving a message to the people. Now concerning your prayer language or private prayer language you have control over volume and the speed at which you speak but not the content. You are speaking in an unknown tongue to you. You can't understand it and neither can the devil understand it. So how do you check yourself? (I'm glad you asked). This is how simple it is and that is; if you can understand it so can the devil and you are absolutely not praying in your prayer language. Praying in your prayer language is from you directly to God. The Holy Spirit of God takes exactly what you are saying to God and makes it exactly what you should be saying for your needs from God at that moment. Although you might think you know what you really need from God. But I submit to you that if you don't know the future, you don't really know what you need from God. This is one reason why you should give the Holy Spirit of God an opportunity to assist you and work on your behalf because this is the Holy Spirit of God job so don't mess with it. Ask Him to assist you and he is more than happy to do so. The devil understands every language under the sun or in the world except your prayer language or private prayer language (which is the same) spoken by you directly to God. If you speak in tongues, you will need an interpretation for the people. When you interpret, the devil will also understand it. So your prayer language is very important. It's from you directly to God. Why do you think the devil is so angry, putting thoughts in the minds of people to forbid or forbidding the practice of praying in your prayer language by Christians? You are speaking in an unknown tongue or prayer language that God have kept for his understanding only. The Holy Spirit of God takes what you are saying and presents it to God for exactly what you need from God. This is far better than a computer trying to print out your future or needs. I'll tell you again that you might think you know what you need from God but the Holy Spirit of God knows your future and knows exactly, at the right time and moment of what you need from God. This is one reason why your private prayer language or your prayer language is so important for you. Don't let anyone stop you from enjoying this privilege and opportunity to be blessed by God. You can't go wrong with God. It's impossible to go wrong with God.

THINK FOR REAL ....

KEEP IT SIMPLE ....

45. Sing

Sing ……………. May refer to: singing, the act of producing musical sounds with the voice, contents, music. To utter a series of words or sounds in musical tones. To vocalize songs or selections. God have blessed you with a voice. Sing to God. You don't have to be a pro. Just make some sounds for him. He will like that. But remember: just because you don't see him, feel him, touch him, hear him, smell him, or since him don't mean he is not listening to you. He is God and never gets tired of hearing from you. You have no idea how much he want you and want to hear from you. If you only knew……..

Singing ……………… Singing is the act of producing musical sounds with the voice, and augments regular speech by use of both tonality and rhythm. One who sings is called a singer. Singing is the one talent virtually everybody possesses. Of course, some are more naturally skilled than others, but even a poor voice can be a singer. You are just not singing the pro stuff but you don't have to be a pro to qualify to be a singer. The truth is, God love your singing and sounds to him greatly if you are singing to Him. He can't wait to hear from you. This is one of the reasons why he made you so he can enjoy you. He needs it and wants it because it is coming from you. If you truly want to become a great singer for your Lord and savior Jesus Christ, you must practice using your singing voice. It is okay if you aren't sure of what to do when you practice your singing. Make a joyful noise to the Lord. If you are doing it for him, He loves every part of your singing to him because it is coming from you who he loves. Be smart and keep it simple.

46. Life

Life .... The ability to grow, change, etc., which separates plants and animals from things like water or rocks. The period of time when a person is alive, the experience of being alive. God is life. He breathes life into man in the beginning and it never stopped. Except when it is your time to cease to live. Everyone have to reach this point someday. Never feel bad or sorry full when you get to this point if you plan to go to heaven. Likewise, you have all the reasons to feel sad if you plan to go to hell. You cannot choose both. It has to be one or the other. You can't run or hide from it. If you plan to go to heaven, God is more than ready to receive you because He has waited for a long time to enjoy you face to face. Never worry about those you leave behind. If God took care of you, he will do the same for them if they let Him. So, the day is going to come, like it or not, you can't run or hide from it. Choose wisely.

THINK FOR REAL ....

Human life .... Human life or simply life may refer to, in philosophy, the human condition or "condition Humana" personal life. Human life is that which God breathe into the nostrils of man in the start of man's time as alive. Human life is that which God have given to mankind to be able to exist for a set time that only God knows. For God states that a man's life is not his own. It belongs to God. For whoever finds God finds life because He is life. Whoever loves God loves life. God is life. You can never go wrong with God. It's a blessing that He does not charge us for life. We don't have to purchase it.

47. Creative Miracle

Creative Miracle .... Impartation one of the gifts of the Holy Spirit, is the working of miracles. God said; "let there be light!" Light includes the entire electromagnetic spectrum. A creative miracle is when God does the impossible according to human beings standards. But it is written that nothing is impossible for God. This is another reason why we should keep things simple. If we could do what God does why will we ever need Him? We do our part with the power God gives us and then God does his part. If you are real with God He will be real with you. If you are false with God he will choose not to hear you and you will fail because the devil will make sure you do. Creative miracle means a healing which involves the sudden appearance of something that previously did not exist. I believe that God wants to raise our faith to level that creative miracles are normal events in our lives and really believe strongly that if your faith is as small as a grain of muster seed and you take action on the word you say or speak, the Holy Spirit of God will do his part after you complete everything in the Name of Jesus. So remember, (The Holy Spirit of God does the work after you say thank you Jesus for it or simply, in the Name of Jesus). So it's (by the power of the Holy Spirit of God in the Name of Jesus). Keep it simple and you can't go wrong. Suddenly as the Lord released a creative miracle, ear drums were formed on the inside of her head and her hearing was opened for the first time in her life. Understand that it is not necessary for us to know all the technical details of how that happened. Jesus already made it very easy for us. He said that it is the Holy Spirit of God job. It is in your best interest to let the Holy Spirit do his job. Our part is easy and simple. So keep it simple, speak the word and let the Holy Spirit of God do his part. Don't for get to say

"Thank you Jesus for it". This makes your task complete. Always complete your task. If you don't see your positive results, say Holy Spirit of God I thank you for my positive results in Jesus Name. Thank You for doing it for me in Jesus Name. (You can say this until you receive-if you want).

48. Creative

Creative .... having or showing an ability to make new things or think of new ideas, using the ability to make or think of new things, involving the process by which new things are brought into existence. Resulting from originality of thought, expression, etc., imaginative, creative writing, originative, productive (usually followed by a solution). Creativity is a phenomenon where by something new is created (such as an idea, a joke, an artistic or literary work), a painting or musical composition. Creative commons helps you share your knowledge and creativity with the world. Creative commons develops, supports, and stewards legal and technical. God give man the ability to be creative. God Himself made male and female. He blessed them and said to them "Be fruitful and increase in number, fill the earth and subdue it. Rule over the fish of the sea and the birds of the air and over every living creature that moves on the ground." God give man the creativity to rule over the entire earth and everything in it. Because the devil is on the earth with man doesn't give you a right to let him take control. Know your rights and take charge of it.

THINK FOR REAL ....

49. More on Miracle

More on miracle .... A miracle is an event that appears inexplicable by the laws of nature and so is held to be supernatural in origin or an act of God. Miracles are spontaneous; they cannot be reproduced by man. It comes directly from God. He can do it as much as He wants and does it all around the world we live in. He never fails to do it for his people. Enquiry concerning human understanding of a miracle by God shows that we are not keeping things simple. We want to do the job of the Holy Spirit of God which we will never be able to do. But God is all for us being blessed by it and enjoying the results of what He has done for us. The results are always good. This is another reason why as humans we need to do our part and leave the hard parts to God where it belongs. If we mess with the hard parts, the devil will keep us going after that and accomplish his goal to keep us away from serving God. He will give you all the reason why God wants you to do that but remember that this hard part is for the Holy Spirit of God. It is so simple for Him. If you are a doctor or scientist or people of such nature who loves getting into such hard things; ask the holy Spirit of God to show you what to do and thank Him for doing it in Jesus Name and watch success-ful results come your way. God loves doctors, scientists, and people of such nature. If they only knew how much God wants to show them ways to make things come easy for them and not take years or their lifetime on a given task, they will give him an opportunity to share with them. Believe it or not, He will never charge them to share information on their task. He is more than happy and willing to see them gain positive results. Make yourself available and understanding to grab a hold of God's sharing. You don't use it, you lose it. It's all up to you. No one is going to make you do it.

50. Taking of Your Own Life

Taking Of Your Own Life .... What does the bible say about taking of your own life? Or, do you not know that your body is a temple of the Holy Spirit within you, whom you have from God? You are not your own, for you were bought with a price. Taking of your own life hurts your love ones and others who care about you. For many, depression is a silent and painful experience. Please do not listen to everything your thoughts tell you. If it is not from your heart, don't do it. If your mind wouldn't let you listen to your heart, go get help. Correct this before you take your next step to act. If you are feeling suicidal, or want to end your life, it's important that you keep yourself safe. Try to remember that thoughts about taking of your life are not from God. It's from the devil. How do you know this is true? (I'm glad you asked). Your answer is: It is not part of God's job description. But we know that it is part of the devil job description. Just because you can't see him, feel him, smell him, hear him, touch him, or even know who he is don't mean he is not there with you. He is messing with your mind. Stop listening to your mind and listen to your heart only at this point. If you are not able to listen to your heart don't ever kill yourself. Go get help. It's not as bad as you think. Do you think to take your own life is the coward's way out or do you think it takes guts? No matter how you think or feel about this, always listen to your heart because your mind is playing tricks on you at the moment and your mind is where all the problems are being pushed around. You can't at this moment trust it. God tells us that taking of your own life is one of the sins that He never forgives. Anyway you view this it comes down to the final point; "IT'S NOT YOURS TO TAKE OR KILL". It is only given to you by God so you can enjoy life and live for God. You are just a care taker of it. You've never purchased one before and you will never be able to purchase one. You've gotten so used to it until you are thinking it's yours and you have always had it. You have never asked yourself how much did you pay for it? Or where can you purchase another one if you destroy this one you have? However, you are missing one valuable point; how did you get life into your body? What did you do to acquire life in your body? Think for real and keep it simple. If you can't answer these questions find the nearest help possible to start working with you on this problem. Force yourself to get to someone for help first if your mind will not let you listen to your heart as a way of check and balance.

51. Suicide

Suicide .... (To kill oneself) Is the act of intentionally causing one's own death. Suicide is often carried out as a result of despair. Suicide prevention starts with recognizing the warning signs and taking them seriously. Whether you're considering suicide or know someone who feels suicidal, learn what you can do about suicide warning signs and how to reach out for immediate help and professional help. Help is very important at this point because God does not forgive this sin. As Christians we should be willing to bind the devil and cast out the spirit of suicide and death out of the individual's mind and body according to Mark 11:23 and command Life to come back into their minds and body in Jesus Name. Thank the Holy Spirit of God for coming and living inside of the individual and renewing his or her mind. Speak the peace of God in their life, mind, and body immediately. It's not our problem how God is going to do it. It is very important to remember this because you need not try to make anything happen. You are always welcome to repeat your part if you choose to. You have done your part and God is well able to handle his business in doing his part. We stay ready for the positive results. We speak our part and He does his part. Keep it simple. Stick to your part. Think for real. We all feel overwhelmed by difficult emotions or situations sometimes. If someone is seriously depressed, suicidal thinking is a real concern at this stage. Consider this as an early warning sign and start the help process. Get them some help today, not tomorrow or the end of the week, or when you can find some time. Make the time now, not later. You can start with the nearest available suicide prevention and mental health service provider in your local area. If things get out of hand or control before you can take action, stay with the individual and call your local police department at 911 for immediate help. Don't turn away for a second. Keep an eye on the individual until help arrives. Don't turn away for a second.

THINK FOR REAL ………………..

52. Blasphemy Against the Holy Spirit of God

Blasphemy against the Holy Spirit of God ....
The act or offense of speaking sacrilegiously about God or sacred things; profane talk. Therefore I say to you, any sin and blasphemy shall be forgiven men, but blasphemy against the Spirit shall not be forgiven. The definition of blasphemy is: saying something concerning God that is very disrespectful. (A good rule to follow: if you have nothing good to say to or about God or anyone else, keep your mouth shut until you can find something nice to say). A contemptuous or profane act, utterance, or writing concerning God or a sacred entity. The act of claiming for oneself the attributes and rights of God. Impious utterance or action concerning God. The act of insulting or showing contempt or lack of reverence for God. The term can be applied to such signs as cursing God or willfully degrading things of God. Whoever blasphemes against the Holy Spirit never has forgiveness in this age or the age to come. If you are Saying bad things about His Name (Jesus), you can be forgiven, but blasphemy the Holy Spirit, or against the Holy Spirit, whoever blasphemes (speaks against) the Holy Spirit will never be forgiven for God's Holy Spirit is constantly urging us to repentance, holiness and salvation. Overt, verbal, and conscious repudiation of the fact that God is not at work in us, urging us to repent, receive salvation, and stay holy is blasphemy against the Holy Spirit of God. These are sins which will not be forgiven by God. It is written.....
But whoever blasphemes against the Holy Spirit will never be forgiven, but is guilty of an unforgivable sin. Blasphemy against the Holy Spirit of God is beyond – forgiveness. Whoever does the will of God is my brother, and sister, and

mother but whoever blasphemes against the Holy Spirit never has forgiveness in this life or the life there after. However, blasphemy against the Holy Spirit is a perpetual, constant resisting of the drawing love of God's Spirit, so that you lose the capacity to hear the Holy Spirit of God. At this point we can come to a quick decision and say so far there are only two sins that God say are unforgivable. (1) Blasphemy against the Holy Spirit of God and (2) The taking of your own life (suicide). So we can also say that other sins are forgivable if you are still alive to repent and take action on your repentance but note that: GOD DID NOT TAKE AWAY THE PRICE YOU WOULD HAVE TO PAY FOR COMMITING THOSE SINS. Note also that Jesus took all these forgivable sins with Him to the cross and left them there where they belong, away from people. Anytime you reach out and take one of these sins from on the cross and use it you will have to pay the price that come with it and it's on your own head. You do the crime, you do the time. Jesus did his part and you must at all cost do your part. The best and safest thing to do is leave those sins back on the cross and don't mess with them. They do bite back. While Pharisees cannot deny the reality of the miracle, they chose to deny that it came from God. This also is blasphemy against the Holy Spirit of God which results in the unpardonable sin. God does not share his glory with anyone. God give you everything but kept this for Himself. Don't be greedy. Leave this one for him. You can't spend it and will not even miss it. You'll never be able to use it to get rich or gain wealth. Give God the glory always. Blasphemy (Catholic Encyclopedia) "to injure, and pheme, reputation, signifies etymologically gross irreverence towards any person or thing worth of exalted esteem. Blasphemy is the act of insulting or showing contempt or lack of reverence for deities, to religious or holy persons or things, or towards something considered holy. As Christians we believe that no one can be exalted to the level of God, The Holy Spirit of God, and Jesus Christ our Lord. Think for real

...... even the devil cannot be on the same level with God. He was created by God. With all the power that God let him keep when he was kicked out of heaven he still can't be on the same level with God. As Christians we can defeat the devil by using the power of God. Take note of what you have within you that you are not using. Learn to use it now.

THINK FOR REAL ....

What should you be doing while someone is praying for you or ministering to you? (I'm glad you asked). While someone is praying for you ....

1. Keep your mouth shut. You cannot receive and transmit at the same time. Someone has to do the listening in order to agree with or disagree with. Both can't be talking at the same time.

2. If you hear something during prayer that is meaningful to you or that you are in agreement with, it is okay to make a response.

3. Listen to what is being said to you or on your behalf. You may agree by making a response or disagree by saying nothing at all. Or silently to yourself, I don't agree with that.

When finished being prayed for, remember to thank Jesus for the prayer and the parts that you agree with. You may say an Amen for agreement and thankfulness.

While   someone   is   ministering   to   you
....

1. If being ministered to for a certain illness, listen to what is being said on your behave.

2. Keep your eyes open. Or, you will miss the miracle as it is happening or taking place. Just think about what it would have been like if they wrote the bible with their eyes closed.

3. Thank Jesus for your healing for whatever healing is being called into existence on your behalf. This is not the time for you to agree or disagree. This is the time to stay in agree-

ment with the person who is ministering to you. (no exceptions)

4. Listen to what is being said and follow the commands being given to you. Never say I can't or I'm unable to do that. No one said you could, however, if you fail to take action on what you are asked to do, your results rest on your own head. Making an attempt to; is a great place to start. Remember, you do your part, and then God does his part. You do nothing to follow the commands given, not even a slight effort, you get nothing. Like it or not, this is real life. You must take action. Even if you reach for someone and say please help me move, or what's asked of you.

5. Keep your mouth shut while being ministered to and your eyes open and respond only when asked to do so.

6. At the end of your session always say ("thank you Jesus for my healing"). Never, never, never ever leave this out. This is faith in action.

7. When you are giving a command to do something don't say I can't do it. If you want God to do his part you must do your part. Take action on what's being commanded of you by putting your faith in action. (Simply means: start first, that's it). Physically doing what is asked of you. Make an attempt even if you think or know you can't move or do what is asked of you to do. Note: You or no one can make anything happen for you but by putting your faith in action you leave no room for God to allow you to win over him. God will never allow you to get the upper hand, meaning that, He must win and show you, the world, and those with unbelief that He is God and will remain your God at any cost. There is nothing you can do about that.

8. Note that; from the start of ministering to you, the power of the Holy Spirit of God is already going or gone into your body and working on your behalf. This is one of the most important parts to know and understand.

9. In some cases just because you don't see anything instant happening at that moment when you are being ministered to doesn't mean the Holy Spirit of God is not working on your behalf. This is the number one error that causes many people to lose their healing. Don't join that number of people. Know He is and thank him for your positive results. Give him the Glory for it. Stay smart.

Stay the course and believe God for your healing by taking action on what is being asked of you and said on your behave.

THINK FOR REAL ....

What should you be doing after you have been prayed for or ministered to? (I'm glad you asked).

1. You should know and understand that from the time you were prayed for or ministered to, the power of the Holy Spirit of God has already started working in you. (Note: Just because you don't feel anything at present, don't mean He's not working in you).

2. Thank the Holy Spirit of God in Jesus Name for the answers to your prayers or for your healing.

3. If any symptoms (real or false or phantom) appears, make sure to speak the word against it. Example: You symptom of _? , right now in Jesus Name and by the power of the Holy Spirit of God, come out and stay out. I thank you Jesus for looking over your world to perform it for me. If you think or you are not sure if the devil had anything to do with it, cast it out any way. It will hurt nothing if nothing is there to be cast out but if something is still there it will have nowhere to run or hide but to obey your commands. Example: Devil I bind you and break your power right now, I cut off your power in Jesus Name and by the power of the Holy Spirit of God, I thank You Holy Spirit for taking action on the words I have spoken for a positive result in Jesus Name.

4. Know and understand that all answers to prayers or healings after being ministered to are not always instant results. (This will save your life, get your prayers answered, and see your healing come true). The Lord decides if it should be instant or to take a little more time. His reasons are always prefect. Wait to hear from Him.

5. Continue to thank Jesus each day for the answers to your prayers or for your healing after you have been ministered to. Remember that you can never, never, never, never, say too much of thank You Jesus. I will wear it out if I had to. (Why is that? I'm glad you asked). Saying thank you Jesus is faith in action. You are actually telling Jesus that I know you have already healed me or you have answered my prayers. I'm just waiting for everybody else to see what You have done for me. This is part of what makes God move on your behave. This is faith in action. Note: At this point, God is looking at you and saying well now, thanks for trying but I just can't let you do more than me because I am God, so I'm going to give you instant results or one week wait or up to a month to have everything fully completed for you. Only God decides that. Like it or not.

6. Maintain your healing or continue to believe for your answers to your prayers. Everyone thinks that because it is God, everything should be instant. However, if your doctor said to you take this pill for the next week or for the next month and come back for checkup you will do just what he said and your mind will line up with his instructions so why not give God the same respect and an opportunity to work on your behalf the way he wants to? Note: Don't go around making statements like; I have been prayed for by the best; TV ministers, preachers, great men and women of God, and etc., but they all failed to get me whole. You are speaking with your own mouth exactly what you are getting. There is no faith in action present. Thanks to you, you are destroying everything they have asked God to do for you. Remember,

that it is not their job to make things happen for you. They did their part to speak the word over you and you also have your part to do which is; Thank you Jesus for your completion of my request, and Jesus have His part to do which is look over his Word to perform it for you. Also remember that every company or business have rules and regulations to follow. The bible is no different. You can't do anything you want. If you don't follow the rules and regulations of the bible and do what your men and women of God tell you to do, don't try to pass your problems and troubles on to them because they have done their part. Now if you are trying to force them to make things happen for you, you will be completely out of line and they will deal with you. When are you going to do your part?

THINK FOR REAL...
KEEP IT SIMPLE ....

53. Check Point # 9

Check Point # 9 .... How do you defeat and
rob a strong man? (I'm glad you asked). Think smart because I
will hate to hear that you got beat-up or killed by such a strong
man or a big strong man. Matthew 12:29, How can anyone
enter a strong man's house and carry off his possessions
unless he first ties up the strong man? Then he can rob his
house. Note: (1) It is best if you don't mess with the strong
man at all. (2) If you find yourself missing with him, make
sure you cover his eyes because if he sees you that might be
the end of you when he come looking for you. Remember the
old saying that you can run but you can't hide forever. You
have to come out for air sometime and you just might get
caught. Now let's apply this to the devil with all that power
that God allowed him to keep. (Keep it simple. The Holy
Spirit of God has all the power you will ever need to defeat the
devil and he does all the hard work for you). You might say
something like this: devil, I bind you and your angels who are
messing with me and what I am concerned about. I break your
power and cut them off by the power of the Holy Spirit of God
in Jesus Name and I command you and your angels to go to
the pits of hell and stay away from me right now in Jesus
Name. (After this; say whatever else you want to say and
conclude by saying; thank you Jesus for doing it for me.
Thank you for looking over your Word to perform it for me).
You can also find scriptures that you can speak on your
situation. And always end in saying; thank you Jesus for doing
it for me.

54. Check Point # 10

Check Point # 10 ……………….. What happens to you when your prayers are not answered, your healing failed to produce positive results, or you are defeated by the devil, or the strong man? Remember that most of these things start in the spiritual realm where you cannot see them or detect them and by the time they become physical for you to see them or notice them they have already started causing problems and damages. Many things can happen or be the cause of your lack of, failure, and defeat. However, we know that most of these things start in the spiritual realm so in keeping things simple, let us look at Matthew 12:43 – 45.

(43) When an evil spirit comes out of a man, it goes through arid places seeking rest and does not find it.

(44) Then it says, I will return to the house I left. When it arrives, it finds the house unoccupied, swept clean, and put in order.

(45) Then it goes and takes with it seven other spirits more wicked than itself, and they go in and live there. And the final condition of that man is worse than the first. This is how it will be with this wicked generation.

We know for a fact that our generation believes in anything that feels good or sounds good to them. They have no cares if things lines up with the Word of God. Everyone is doing their own thing. If God does not hear your prayers, or your commands made for your healing, because you have not clear the gap or open a path for Him to hear you, the results will be negative. If you are doing your own things and serving other things, God will not hear you. But the devil is all eyes and ears and is ready to stop your blessings God have already sent to you or stopped your healings that God have already allowed to happen. If you want everything God got for you,

you must line yourself up with the Word of God. It is very easy to receive from God if you know how to follow instructions and take action on what He tells you to do. In general, that's it. Keep it simple.

55. Check Point # 11

Check Point # 11 .... At this point we need to re-state a few things that you need to understand and watch what you do every day of your life. We know that Jesus died for our sins and took all of our sins on Himself. We also know that we need not part-take in those sins any longer. If we ever reach out and take one of those sins, there will be a price to pay for that. God did not take away the price you have to pay if you jump back into one of these sins that Jesus already removed from our path. God also states that only two sins I do not forgive; taking of your own life and blasphemy against the Holy Spirit of God. So it is safe to say that every other sin is forgivable but not the price you have to pay for messing with those sins that Jesus already removed from your path. You can't come to your pastors and say you prayed for me, told me I'm forgiven, but you never told me if I do this again I will have to pay a price. You've failed me, after all the funds I've paid into this ministry. I no longer trust you, I want my funds back. (Your pastors can handle their business). You also have an opportunity to repent for these sins you took back from Jesus and put to use. All the careless words that you speak to justify your use of those sins will not help you. Not everyone get an opportunity to repent and turn away from messing with those sins. For those who make it, what do you think your future will look like with those prices attached to you? A simple rule to follow is: If you do good for any reasons, you will have a price to pay to do so and if you do bad or wrong, you will still pay a price to do so. If you are going to pay a price anyway, why not just do good? God will always repay you for the good you do. Let's look at Matthew 12:30-32, 36, and 37.

(30) He who is not with me is against me, and he who does not gather with me scatters.

(31) And so I tell you every sin and blasphemy will be forgiven men, but the blasphemy against the Spirit will not be forgiven.

(32) Anyone who speaks a word against the son of man will be forgiven, but anyone who speaks against the Holy Spirit will not be forgiven, either in this age or in the age to come.

(36) But I tell you that men will have to give account on the Day of Judgment for every careless word they have spoken.

(37) For by your words you will be acquitted, and by your words you will be condemned.

56. Check Point # 12

Check Point # 12 .... It is always right and a good thing to speak the truth. However it still comes with a price attached to it. This old saying; the truth will set you free does not leave out the attached price to it. Telling the truth about the wrong you did can send you to prison or death or pay fines. So knowing all this, it is best to say that the truth that you believe will set you free because your mind, body, and spirit is in agreement to pay the price attached to it. But have no fear if you are serving God because, the Holy Spirit of God will dispatch your angel on your behalf to protect you from all harm, hurt, and danger and you will have an opportunity to continue the work God have called you to do. Stay smart, your future is still ahead of you. Do the right things and tell the truth.

57. Example # 3

Example # 3 .... Making the scriptures personal to you and allowing it to come alive in your life daily. So what are we really doing at this point? (I'm glad you asked). We are taking our needs, wants, desire of our hearts, etc., and the list goes on and lining them up with the scriptures and speaking them on our behalf. We are also calling things that are not as thou they were. We are speaking life into our situation and thanking God for looking over his Word to perform them in our lives. You have to speak it with your mouth, not your mind or your thinking. By hearing yourself speak, (make sure it is really you doing the speaking and stay away from spooky stuff) you are renewing your mind which encourages you to take action on what you are speaking and hearing yourself say. The Word of God is alive and real. It is just waiting for you to put it to use. It will give you a different way of reading your Bible and believing God for what you want and claiming the promises God has for you in His Word and thanking him for making them come to pass for you. Your future is still ahead of you. The best is still yet to come in your path. Stay smart, keep it simple and listen for the voice of the Holy Spirit of God who is going to teach you all truths and show you all hidden riches waiting for you to take. Remember that the Holy Spirit of God have done all the hard and difficult parts and task so if you are confused or finding things complex and difficult, make sure that it is from God before you move on. Do that by checking to see what the word of God have to say about that. Now let's start with:

A. Psalms 91, then add Mark 11:22-25. Read it and understand it. Find your scriptures and do one of your own.

B. Proverbs 3:1-6, 1 Samuel 2:26, Luke 2:52, Numbers 14:28, 1 Corinthians 15:58, Proverbs 18:20-21, and Luke 1:25-28. Find your scriptures and do one of your own.

C. Luke 6:38, Find your scriptures and do one of your own.

D. Find your scriptures and do one of your own.

E. Psalms 91:11, Luke 2:14, Daniel 6:16, Isaiah 43:26, Isaiah 55:11, and Psalms 2:8. Find your scriptures and do one of your own.

F. 1 Peter 5:8-11, 2 Peter 1:10-11. Find your scriptures and do one of your own.

G. Find your scriptures and do one of your own.

H. Psalms 35:1-28. Find your scriptures and do one of your own.

Isaiah 54:9-17, Deuteronomy 8:18, Jeremiah 33:3, Romans 11:29, 2 Corinthians 10:3-5, 2 Corinthians 9:6-15. Find your scriptures and do one of your own.

(A) I who dwells in the shelter of the most high will rest in the shadow of the Almighty. I will say of the Lord, He is my refuge and my fortress, my God, in whom I trust. Surely He has saved me from the fowler's snare and from the deadly pestilence. He has covered me with his feathers, and under his wings I have found refuge; His faithfulness is my shield and rampart. I do not fear the terror of night, nor the arrow that flies by day, nor the pestilence that stalks in the darkness, nor the plague that destroys at midday. A thousand may fall at my side, ten thousand at my right hand, but it will not come near me. I will only observe with my eyes and see the punishment of the wicked. The Most High is my dwelling------The Lord is my refuge------no harm will befall me, no disaster will come near my house. For He will command his angels concerning me to guard me in all my ways; they will lift me up in their hands, so that I will not strike my foot against a stone. I am treading upon the lion and the cobra; I am tramping the great lion and the serpent. Because the Lord loves me, He has rescued me; He is protecting me, for I acknowledge His Name. As he calls upon me, I am answering Him; He will be with me if I am in trouble, He is delivering me and honoring me. With long life will He satisfy me and show me His Salvation.

According to Mark 11:22 through verse 25 I thank You Lord Jesus for looking over your Word to perform it at all times for me. I thank you Holy Spirit of God for dispatching my angel to execute promptly every word out of my mouth as You look over your word to perform it. I thank you Holy Spirit of God for this overcoming power I have because of You in Jesus Name. I thank You for living inside of me and causing me to perform every miracle that God has ordained for my life. Right now in Jesus Name I say to every mountain in my life, go, throw yourself into the sea, and with no doubt in my heart but truth and strong believes that what I've said is happening and is being done for me every day. Therefore, whatever I ask for in prayer, I believe that I have received it in Jesus Name and it is mine. And as I stand commanding, if I hold anything against anyone, forgive me Lord so that Your Father in Heaven may forgive me my sins. I speak life into every word that comes out of my mouth every day in Jesus Name. I thank you Jesus for looking over your word to perform it as I call things that are not as though they were. I thank you Holy Spirit of God for the angels of God and my angel that are assign to me to carry out every command out of my mouth as it lines up with the Word of God and his Will for my life. I thank you for your blessings Lord Jesus, Amen.

(B) Lord Jesus, I thank you for forgiving me for my sins as I forgive those that have sinned against me. I also thank you for this breakthrough to you. Holy Spirit of God, I thank you for living inside of me and causing me to have favor with God and men in Jesus Name. Father, I thank you for looking over your word to perform it in my life daily. I thank you for giving me favor with God and men as I call things that are not as thou they were, as I am calling and speaking things into existence. Father, according to proverbs 3:1-6, I thank you, I do not forget your teachings and I keep your commands in my heart because they prolong my life for many years and brings me prosperity. I thank you Holy Spirit of God for making sure that love and faithfulness never leave me as I bind them around my neck and write them on the tablet of my heart in Jesus Name. I win favor and a good name every day in the sight of God and man in Jesus Name. I trust in you Lord with all my heart and I lean not on my own understanding. In all my ways I acknowledge you Lord and you make my paths straight. I thank you Father in Jesus Name that I've continued to grow in stature and in favor with you Lord and with men, according to 1 Samuel 2:26 as you look over your Word to perform it every day of my life. I thank you Holy Spirit of God in Jesus Name for causing me to grow in wisdom and stature, and in favor with God and men according to Luke 2:52. I also thank you Lord Jesus for Numbers 14:28 as your Word tells me that you will do to me the very things you hear me say, so Holy Spirit of God, I thank you for guiding and directing me in the path of righteousness. I thank you Holy Spirit of God in Jesus Name for helping me to stand firm, letting nothing move me as I always give myself fully to the work of the Lord because I know that my labor in the Lord is not in vain according to 1 Corinthians 15:58. Father I thank you in Jesus Name that from the fruit of my mouth, my stomach is filled and with the harvest from my lips I am satisfied according to proverbs 18:20-21. I also thank you Holy Spirit of God in Jesus Name that you have done this for me. In these days, you have shown your favor and taken away my disgrace among the people. I thank you that you have caused me to find favor with God and men as the angel of the Lord greets me because I am Highly favored before you Lord as he tells me, the Lord is with me according to Luke 1:25-28. I thank you Lord Jesus for looking over your Word to perform them in my life daily. I command all these words to line up with the Word of God I have spoken in the Name of Jesus as I press forward toward my goals, and hearts desires in this life and the life here after. Amen.

(C) Father, I'm standing on Luke 6:38 which says, give and it shall be given unto me, good measure , pressed down, shaken together, running all over the place, shall men give unto my bosom. Father, my family and I have given over and over. I call into being this verse of scripture right now for the finances of more than enough for my family and me. In Jesus Name, thank you for looking over your Word and performing it for us. I claim it, I expect it, I except it, I believe it, I take action on it, I speak it right now into existence, I believe every word of Luke 6:38 for my finances by faith in Jesus Name as I take action on Luke 6:38. Thank you Father for supernaturally performing your Word and making it come to pass in the natural for my finances. Thank you Holy Spirit of God for dispatching my angel to minister to me and every need that I have. I also thank you for my wants and hearts desires as your word promise. Thank you Holy Spirit of God for helping me to condition myself and line myself up to be blessed continuously, as I place myself in a position to be blessed by obeying your Word. I thank you Jesus for doing this for me. Amen.

(D) Thank you Jesus for forgiving me for my sins as I forgive those that have sinned against me. Thank you for this breakthrough to you. Father, in the Name of Jesus, I thank you that you created angels, and for such exciting purposes. Thank you that you sent an angel down to protect Shadrach, Meshach, Abednego and _ (your name here) __ right in the middle of our fiery furnace. We didn't even get burned and we didn't even smell like smoke because the angel you sent protected us. I thank you Lord that this same protection rest upon me, in Jesus Name. Oh Father, How I thank you that you protected Daniel in the lion's den. Thank you that you sent Gabriel down to explain the vision to Daniel so that things he didn't understand were revealed through the angel who brought a message directly from your lips. Father, I thank you for Philips, too. I thank you that he heard when an angel of the Lord spoke. I thank you that when the angel said, "go near" he got over there and did what you wanted him to do, and that was to present the plan of salvation to the Ethiopian Eunuch! Father, I ask you in the Name of Jesus to lose the vast armies of heaven to bring my love ones and total families to a person, to a point, or to a place where they will find the living Jesus, where they will find Jesus as their Savior and Lord. I thank you right now! Thank you Holy Spirit of God for dispatching angels and for sending them out on duty. I thank you that those angels are going to do miracles in the lives of my love ones and total families as I rejoice even now. My heavenly Father, the next time I see one of my family who is not saved, I am going to smile to myself and say, "you don't even know that you've got angels all around you shoving you right towards that person who is going to lead you to salvation. Halleluiah! I asked this in the Name of Jesus! Thank you for answering my prayer Father in Jesus Name. Amen.

(E) I thank you Jesus for forgiving me for my wrong doings as I forgive those that have wronged me. I thank you for this breakthrough to you. I thank you Father for my angel that is assigned to me and that angels are in charge of me. I am surrounded by angels at all times who ministers to me and protect me and my family even from accidents and losses of any kind that concerns us. I am accompanied by angels, defended by angels, and preserved by them because you have ordered them to do so according to Psalms 91:11. Thank you Father in the Name of Jesus and by the power of the Holy Spirit for choosing to sovereignly, releasing angels into my situation here on earth as it is in heaven. I thank you Holy Spirit of God for dispatching angels that are with me and performing mighty acts on my behalf day and night even without me being aware of their presence. Glory to God in the highest heaven, I sing, and peace on earth for all those pleasing Him according to Luke 2:14. My God is able to save me, and if He chooses to do that, it's great; but if He doesn't chose to save me, that's still great, because regardless, I'm still going to serve Him. My God whom I serve continually, He will and is delivering me according to Daniel 6:16. I thank you Jesus for Isaiah 43:26 which says for me to remind you of your Word. Thank you for allowing me to do this. Also In Isaiah 55:11 you promised me that your Word will not return to you void but will accomplish what you pleases. I thank you that as I speak your Word, You do not let it return to you void. I thank you Holy Spirit of God for making me aware of the activity angels and the sending of angels to do specific things in my life here on earth as it is in heaven and even when I don't know to ask for one in Jesus Name. Holy Spirit of God I thank you for sending someone with the good news of Jesus to each one of my total family whose heart would be willing to receive Jesus, according to Psalms 2:8 as You said to ask of you, and you will give me the nations for my inheritance. Thank you for your Word. Thank you for giving me the nations for my inheritance in Jesus Name.

(F) Lord Jesus, as I come before you this day, I asked that you forgive me for my sins. I also thank you right now for forgiving me right now. I thank you for this breakthrough to you. Holy Spirit of God , I thank you for living inside of me, perfecting me, guiding my footsteps and keeping me from all harm, hurt, and danger. Lord Jesus, I thank you for my angel that you created for me and have given charge over me. Lord you said in your Word that if I will humble myself under the mighty hand of God, in His good time he will lift me up. Thank you for taking all my worries and cares. For You are always thinking about me and watching everything that concerns me. Lord, your word according to 1 Peter 5:8-11 says, be careful, watch out for attacks from Satan, my great enemy. He prowls around like a hungry, roaring lion, looking for some victim to tear apart. Stand firm when he attacks. Trust the Lord and remember that other Christians all around the world are going through these sufferings too. After I have suffered a little while, my God who is full of kindness through Christ, will give me his eternal glory. You personally will come and pick me up, and set me firmly in place and make me stronger than ever. To You be all power over all things, forever and I will work hard to prove that I'm really among those God has called and chosen, and then I will never stumble or fall away. And God will open wide the gates of heaven for me to enter into the eternal kingdom of my Lord and Savior Jesus Christ. 2 Peter 1:10-11. Lord Jesus, I thank you for the care you take to live in me, and let me live in You. You are my vine; You are my branches. Whoever lives in you and you in them shall produce a large crop of fruit. For apart from you I can't do a thing. Lord Jesus, I will stay in you and obey your commands, so I may ask any request I like that lines up with Your word and it will be granted. I am learning to be a true disciple who will produce bountiful harvests for I know that this brings great glory to you Father. Thank you Lord Jesus for choosing me. You appointed me to go and produce lovely fruit always, so that no matter what I asked from you Father, using your name, you will give it to me. Lord Jesus I thank you for sending the comforter—the Holy Spirit of God, He's the source of all truths. He has come from the Father, He lives inside of me and tells me all about you Lord Jesus because you have been with the Holy Spirit from the beginning. Lord Jesus, I thank you for being a blessing to me every day of the year. I thank you Lord for the power you have given me to do every work that you have called me to do. I thank you for every part of my body, working, and functioning properly and normally every day. I thank you for love, joy, and peace in Jesus Name. Amen.

(G) According to your Word Lord, this is Jehovah's message to (place your name here), God's anointed whom He has chosen to conquer many lands, problems, situations, and disappointments. My God has empowered my right hand and I shall crush the strength of mighty Kings and any problems I'm faced with. My God has opened up the gates of favor and victory to me and for me; the gates of Babylon shall not be shut against me anymore. I will always defeat all of my enemies daily in Jesus Name. Thank you Lord for going before me and leveling the mountains that I face daily, and smashing down the city gates of brass and iron bars that they will try to use against me. So right now in Jesus Name I thank you Holy Spirit of God for watching over me and showing me all truths. I thank you for giving me treasures hidden in the darkness, for giving me secret riches; and I will know and give you thanks for doing this, my Lord, the God of my life, The One who calls me by my name. I thank you Lord that I am chosen by you for this work. I thank you for strengthening me as my life is in your hands and sending me out to victory even though I don't fully know you like I should, and all the things that I face in this world from east to west, from north to south and throughout the world they will know it is your doings and there is no one else but you Lord. You alone are God. You form the light and make the dark. You send good times and you allow bad. You are the one who does these things. You open up the heavens and let the skies pour out their righteousness. Only you God in Jesus Name lets salvation and righteousness sprout up together from the earth. Lord you say in your Word that the ungodly shall be subject to me. They shall come to me with all their merchandise and it shall all be mine to use for your purpose. They shall follow me as prisoners in chains, and fall down on their knees before me and say, "The only God there is, is the God that I serve, the One and true living God". Let all the world look to you for salvation! For there is no other God but You; a just God and a Savior, no not one! My God, You have sworn by yourself and you will never go back on your Word, for it is true that every knee in all the world shall bow to you, and every tongue shall swear allegiance to your Name. Lord Jesus I thank you for your Word for my life this day. I thank you for looking over your Word to perform it for me. Thank you Lord Jesus for forgiving me for all my wrong doings. Thank you for this breakthrough to you. Holy Spirit of God, thank you for living inside of me, keeping me anointed at all times, performing every work and every miracle in my life daily. I thank you Lord for my angel that watches over me daily as you dispatch him on my behalf. I love you Jesus and I'm learning to love you daily by faith. . Amen.

(H)O Lord, I thank you for contending with those who contend with me; I thank you for fighting against those who fight against me. I thank you Lord for taking up shield and buckler; arising and coming to my aid. I thank you for taking up your brandish spear and javelin against those who pursue me. Thank you for saying to my soul that you are my salvation. May those who seek my life be disgraced and put to shame as you look over your Word to perform it in my life. May those who plot my ruin be turned back in dismay and I thank you Jesus for it. May they be like chaff before the wind, with the angel of the Lord and my angel driving them away. I thank you Lord that their paths are dark and slippery, with the angel of the Lord and my angel pursuing them. Since they hid their nets for me without cause and without cause dug a pit for me, may ruin over take them by surprise. May the nets they hid entangle them and cause them to fall into the pit to their ruin. I thank you Lord Jesus that then my soul will rejoice as I delight in your salvation. As I call things that are not as thou they were, in Jesus Name, I thank you Lord that my whole being is exclaiming, "who is like you, O Lord? You daily rescue the poor from those too strong for them, also the poor and the needy from those who rob them". As ruthless witnesses come forward and question me on things I know nothing about and repay me evil for good and leave my soul for long, in Jesus Name I humble myself before you with fasting and praise and worship to you. I thank you Lord Jesus that my prayers are not returned to me unanswered. I thank you Jesus that I am not bowing my head in grief. But if I stumble or am unaware of my attackers against me I thank you Lord for not looking on but rescuing my life and everything that concerns me from their ravages. I thank you Lord for everything and everywhere I go, among any people I will praise you for not letting those gloat over me who are my enemies. Let not those who hate me without cause or without reason maliciously wink their eyes, not speaking peaceably, or devising false accusations against me as I live in the ways of my LORD on this land. I thank you Holy Spirit of God in Jesus Name for not being silent, living inside of me, causing success for me in everything that concerns me, and arising to my defense in all that pertains to me. I thank you for contending for me, my God and Lord in Jesus Name. I thank you for vindicating me in your righteousness O Lord my God in Jesus Name. I thank you for not letting them gloat over me or think "Aha, just what we wanted"! Or say, we have swallowed him up. I thank you Holy Spirit of God in Jesus Name for dispatching my angel to put to shame and confusion all those who exalt themselves over me. I thank you also that they have caused their own shame and disgrace. May those who delight in my vindication shout for joy and gladness; may they always say, "The Lord be exalted, who delights in the well-being of his servant". My tongue is speaking of your righteousness and of your praises all day long. I thank you Jesus for looking over your Word to perform it in my life every day. Amen.

Lord Jesus, I thank you for forgiving me for my wrong doings as I forgive those that have wronged me. As you look over your Word for my life, I thank you for this breakthrough to you. I also thank you for these parts of Isaiah chapter 54, verse 9 through verse 17 that I have claimed as mine, in the Name of Jesus. As you look over these words to perform them in my daily life, I thank you Holy Spirit of God for success in every area that I'm faced with in Jesus Name. You said to me that this is like the days of Noah, when you swore that the waters of Noah would never again cover the earth. So now I thank you for not being angry with me and not rebuking me as you have sworn to Noah in times gone by. Though the mountains be shaken and the hills be removed, yet your unfailing love for me will not be shaken nor your covenant of peace be removed from my life as I call upon you Lord, You who has compassion on me. In Jesus Name I thank you Holy Spirit of God for building me with stones of turquoise, my foundations with sapphires, and my battlements of rubies. I thank you for making my gates of sparkling jewels and all my walls of precious stones. I thank you that all my sons are being taught by you Lord, and great is my children's peace. In righteousness I am established; Tyranny is far from me, I have nothing to fear. Terror is being far removed, it will not come near me. If anyone does attack me, I know Lord that it is not your doing, But I thank you Father for your Word that says; whoever attacks me will surrender to me in Jesus Name. No weapon forged against me will prevail, and you have refuted every tongue that accuses me. This is my heritage as a servant of the Lord, and this is my vindication from God in Jesus Name, declares the Lord. I thank you Lord Jesus for Deuteronomy chapter 8, verse 18, which states: As I remember you Lord my God, You are the ones who gives me the ability to produce wealth and so confirms your covenant, which you swore to my forefathers, as it is today. I thank you Jesus for confirming this in my life daily. I thank you Lord for your Word according to Jeremiah chapter 33, verse 3, which states that as I call to you, You are answering me and telling me great and unsearchable things I do not know so, I am calling on you now Lord in Jesus Name. Thank you for answering me. I thank you God in the Name of Jesus for your gifts to me and your irrevocable call of me for your purpose according to

Romans chapter 11, verse 29. Lord your word also states in 2 Corinthians chapter 10, verse 3 through 5, that as I live in the world, I do not wage war as the world does. The weapons I fight with are not the weapons of the world. On the contrary, my weapons have divine power to demolish strongholds. In Jesus Name I demolish arguments and every pretension that sets itself up against the knowledge of God, and I take captive every thought to make it obedient to Christ. Also in 2 Corinthians chapter 9, verse 6, through verse 15, as you look over your Word to perform it for me in my daily activities, I give you thanks that I sow generously on every occasion and I reap also generously. I give what I have decided in my heart to give, not reluctantly or under compulsion, for God loves me, a cheerful giver, who God, in the Name of Jesus is able to make all grace abound to me, having all that I need, which causes me to abound in every good work. I thank you Father in Jesus Name as you supply seed to me, the sower, and bread for food, you also supply and increased my store of seed and you have enlarged the harvest of my righteousness. I am made rich in every way so that I can give and be generous on every occasion, and through me your generosity will result in thanksgiving to God in Jesus Name as the Holy Spirit leads and performs every work and every miracle overflowing in many expressions of thanks to God. Because of the service by which I have proved myself, men are praising you God in Jesus Name for the obedience that accompanies my confession of the gospel of Christ, and for my generosity in sharing with them and with everyone else. And as they pray to you Lord Jesus, their hearts are going out to you, because of the surpassing grace God has given me. Thanks be to God for His indescribable gift. Thank you Jesus for looking over your Word to perform it in my life daily. Amen

    THINK FOR REAL ....

58. Opening the Gap

Opening The Gap .... What are we talking about here? (I'm glad you asked). Several things need to take place to open the gap. The gap is the point that you need to keep clear to allow God to hear you and your request. At this point we need to keep things as simple as possible. If you are too spiritual or holy you might miss it. However it is very important to follow the instructions God give us on this topic. What closes the gap? A lot of things do, so let's look at a few. (A) Un-forgiveness (B) Wrong doings to others (C) Attacking your Pastors when God never authorized you to do so (D) Wrong living or holding things against others and wouldn't let go (E) Cheat, steal, and lie, especially when you say I'm sorry that you caught me but I'm not sorry for doing it. Or you know of someone that needs help or assistance and they come to you and you are in a position to help or assist but you tell them to come back later or tomorrow hopping they will find someone else to help because you don't want to do it. The list can go on and on. Remember, we are keeping this as simple as we can. So we want to talk to God or make our request to Him, what should we do first? (I'm glad you asked). We should clear the gap first. How do we do that? (I'm glad you asked again). The old saying is: "you never ask, you'll never know"). Asking is the starting point to your success. Let's start of like this: Lord Jesus, I thank you for forgiving me for my sins or wrong doings as I forgive those that have sinned against me or wronged me. I thank you right now for this breakthrough to you. Now you can pray your prayer or make your request unto God after this because you have now opened the gap so God will hear your prayer or request to him.

59. Check Point # 13

Check Point # 13 .... Now remember, keep it simple. If you are looking for something Hi-Tech., you are on the wrong page. Okay, God instruction is clear and simple. He said; if you hold something against your brother or sister (others) and you come to me knowing you have your own sins or wrong doings, I will not hear you. (Okay, how many of you have to go to college to understand that?). What do you think your Pastors or preachers, or men and women of God mean when they tell you to repent? Leave those things that are causing you problems or getting you in trouble, ask for forgiveness, change your ways, and forgive others who have wronged you, holding nothing against them. (You might say well pastor, you are a man of God and you can do that so when I get to your level I will be able to do the same). The truth here is: your pastor is a man or a woman first, then secondly, he or she is a man or woman of God and if he or she can do it, you can do it too. No excuse for you. God instruction is not going to change because of you and the way you feel. Now, after you have done your part of forgiving, God sweeten the deal to hear your prayers or your request. He said I too will not remember your sins or wrong doings against others and I will remember your sins no more as far as the east is from the west. (Now if you can't go there in the same day and be back home in time for supper or dinner, whichever you eat at night, it's too far. Don't even think about trying it). So we see that after this, God is ready to hear your prayers and request. A good rule to follow is: If you are not yet operating in the level of your pastors, ministers, men and women of God, and people of such nature, make time to clear the gap before you start saying anything to God. Remember that God can do things anyway He wants to without asking you for permission.

Check Point # 14 .... How do you respond to the findings of your doctor when he tells you "the virus you are concerned about has spread through all parts of your body and there is nothing we can do for you at this stage? Remember that most of these things starts of in the spiritual realm and by the time your doctor see them, they are all running loose in your body doing what they do best, destroying your body parts. So after your doctor tells you, (this is like a low blow to the gut that wants to knock you out or off your feet). After such information what do you do? Well at this point your mind is now affected by lots of thinking, fear, feeling sad, mad, angry, and saying to yourself and others that the end is near or here for me. There is nothing I or the doctor can do. No hope for me. My time has come to an end for living here on earth. I am sorry that it has come when I'm not really ready to depart from everyone I know and love, and care about. Okay at this point let's remember to keep it simple. Let's also remember that there are only two players involved at this point and if you know the rules to the game you can beat the game. Let's build on what we have before us. Let's also use a virus or disease like cancer that spreads. God said in His Word that you should be careful of what you are saying because He hears you and will do to you exactly what He hear you say. So if you are saying the right things, that's good for you but if you are saying the wrong things, that's bad for you. Choose to say the right things because it can work for you. God said that He is going to do exactly to you what He hears you saying. Understand that he didn't say what he hear you thinking or thinking about. He said what he hears you saying. Now what do you think can help you at this point? Let's put some things together:

A. Be thankful that the doctor has let you in on the problem.

B. Tell God your reason for wanting to stay longer on the earth and giving up going to a beautiful place like Heaven, if that's where you are headed or hell if that is not where you want to go. There are no correct answers that you might think to choose from. It is all about what you really want from God and what you want him to do for you. He is the only one who can tell you if your reason is valet or not. If it is important to you, it is equally important for you to tell God. Never hold back and think that you have to have an excellent reason.

C. No reason that makes sense and lines up with the Word of God goes unheard. We can't say that there are right or wrong reasons because this is between only you and God.

D. Know who the players are for this problem at hand. (Remember that there are only two players).

E. You have only two players: (1) God, ------ He did not give you or sent that, or allowed that virus or disease on you. He is always ready and willing to assist you and heal you. It is not part of His job description to do bad things to you. (2) The devil and his angels, ------ They do not like anything that God like or anything that God made. Part of their job description is to steal, kill, cause problems, put diseases on people, destroy people, and everything negative that you can think of. They really can't help it. It's business as usual for them. That's their job.

F. Knowing who the players are and their job functions helps you think correctly and plan on how you are going to defeat their plans against you and your life.

G. Note that these things start in the spiritual realm. So it is best and a good place for you to start in the spiritual realm speaking the Word of God on your case at hand. After you are done and the positive results shows up in the physical or natural realm, your doctor and others can only say few words, that is; "it's a miracle, it got to be a miracle". Your doctor will say, we can't explain what's going on here but we have the proof of what we saw that is no longer there. Your doctor will also say, we can only at this point keep our eyes on you in case of any future changes. We have no choice but to release you from our care.

Example # 4 .... Do you have any idea how powerful and on time your God is? Do you ever think about how powerful six-eighteen wheelers trucks fully loaded are? Can you imagine all that power put together, running over someone? What part of that person do you believe would be left of him or her on that pavement for someone to say oh look there is (name)? I don't think anyone will be able to say who is on the pavement after those trucks are done with the person. That person might just be as flat as pancakes and unidentifiable. Now keep it simple and let's think about God, Jesus, and the Holy Spirit of God coming and living inside of you and nothing destroys you, your body or your mind and you get to keep your life and continue your daily business as usual. You live to tell about it. The power that made the world and everything there is, on the inside of you and you live without any hurt, harm, or danger to you. Only God can do that. That's one reason why He's God. Even when the devil goes and lives in someone it is just a matter of time before they destroy that person's mind and their body. What reasons will you have at this point to show why your problems stated by your doctor is impossible for your God to take care of for you? (If you know who the players are and you know the rules of the game, you can beat the game). Because Jesus has already given you all the power you will ever need to beat the game and take control. If you don't use it or know how to use it, you lose. If you don't know how, find someone who knows how. So we now go back to this virus or disease (cancer). What do we know about it? How does it function? What does it do to people? Okay, this is the time to make your commands and request unto God. This is not the time for you to pray. You can pray before or after you make your commands and request.

Someone's life may depend on you at this point. Keep your eyes open and don't miss the miracle. Remember to open the gap or make sure it is cleared. This doesn't mean that you have done something wrong. This will not hurt you in any way. If something is there, it will be cleared and if nothing is there, nothing will be cleared. Stay smart and be of good report. Now, let's start like this; Lord Jesus, I thank you for forgiving me and the person I am standing in the gap for, ministering to right now for our sins or wrong doings as we also forgive those that have wronged us or sinned against us. I thank you for this breakthrough to you. Devil, I bind you and your angels of death by the power of the Holy Spirit of God in Jesus Name and I cut off your power over this person right now. I bind and cast out the spirit of cancer. I curse the seeds, roots and cells of the cancer and command them to die and come out in Jesus Name. I command ever affected area and every cancer cell in this body to die in Jesus Name. I command the bone morrow to produce pure healthy blood to every part of this body. In Jesus Name I command healing to all organs and tissues that are affected and restoration of parts where necessary by the power of the Holy Spirit of God in Jesus Name. I command the body's defensive killer cells to multiply and attack all cancer cells and stopping any progressive growths or spreading. I thank you Holy Spirit of God in Jesus Name for a creative miracle of a new immune system in this body. Thank you for putting it in right now. I rebuke any pain in this body right now in Jesus Name and command it to cease and the brain to signal all areas of this body to function properly in Jesus Name. I thank you Holy Spirit of God for taking care of business in Jesus Name. Thank you Jesus for this healing.

Checking Point # 15 .... Don't try to remember everything. Write it down and take it with you and speak it over the person you are ministering to. Stretch out your hand towards the person or affected areas. After you are done, encourage the person to check with their doctor and get back with you. If anything is left, this will be another opportunity for you to attack and beat on the devil some more and get him off this person. Never give up. Someone's life depends on the actions you are taking. If they are not saved, get them saved. Lead them in the prayer to accept Jesus as their personal Lord and Savior. This is not a game. This is real life. We are always at war with the devil. You can't negotiate with him. It is Jesus way or you are dead.

THINK FOR REAL ....

63. Fun Time

Fun Time .... Let's have a little fun at this point. All work and no play is useless. Let's start by saying that in the beginning God created the Heavens and the Earth. (Wish is all true). He created everything there is. (Wish is all true). One day God, Jesus, and the Holy Spirit of God was resting and having a peaceful moment. Let's imagine them on that morning having a donut and drinking coffee. (Your spiritual body needs no food or drink in heaven). Jesus said Father, can I tell you what's on my mind? God said sure son tell me. Jesus said well, we made man in our own image and likeness. For years men have been doing their own things and being distracted by our enemy the devil. The holy men of God we sent to talk to them have not been able to get everything corrected. When these people come before you knowing what they have done or have not done, your presence alone caused them to die. Even the priest had to have a rope tied around him when he came into your presence because if things were not correct and done as you said to do, he will die right on the spot. And the people will have to pull him out from behind the curtain. Father, these people belongs to us too and you are too strong for them. Please let me go down to earth and talk with them to make the necessary corrections as I train them in our ways. They have no idea how much we really love them and want them. We made them to look just the way we look so we can connect and have fun together as we do your Will. Nobody can care for them better than we can. For so many reasons they are not thinking correctly and doing wrong things against our Will for their lives. Father, I got to go down and fix this. God said if you want to take the risk to do that you will have to take the risk on your own. I don't like that idea but I'm not going to stop you from going. Jesus said thank you Father, I will start making plans to go down to earth and win them back to us. (Remember to keep it simple). Now, Jesus can come down to earth because He can change into any form He wants to. This is one reason of the many that makes Him a God. Never forget that. As people we can change too but our changes are limited to forms like big, small, fat, skinny, fine, beautiful, or ugly good, bad, etc. However, because we are not God and have the God power to change into any form we want to, we have to respect the fact that Jesus proved to us that He is God by changing His form to come down to earth and be like us, speak like us, and among other things, train and teach us how to get back in line with their Will for our lives. What Jesus showed us here is that there are two parts to things happening. First part-spiritual and second part – physical. As people we always come in on the physical part because this is the part we get to see first. Now if you are a Christian and allow the Holy Spirit of God to live in you, and work in and through you, you will have opportunities to be alerted by Him to check out the spiritual part and make corrections before thinks become physical or after they become physical He will alert you to check out the spiritual and make corrections as well. So it is up to you to find out how to use this power. ((If you buy a car because you have the money to buy one but don't know how to drive it or even start it, all you would do is get in and sit down on the seat and be going nowhere. Until you connect with those who can teach you and train you to operate the car, you will not be going anywhere in that car. It's best if you get your money back from the dealer if they will be willing to do so). Jesus completed His work here on earth and He said I'm going back to my Father in Heaven but I will not leave you here alone. I will send the Holy Spirit of God back to you and He will be with you forever and he will give you all the power you need to be successful at anything you chose to do as long as it lines up with the Word of God. He will teach you all truths, He will live inside of you, and monitor the earth, he will show you hidden riches, and etc. But He will never force you to do anything. I also want you not to grieve the Holy Spirit of God. So when you are calling Jesus and saying Jesus please come, I need you now. Can you imagine if Jesus was to say why are you calling me when I already give you the Holy Spirit of God to take care of you? He is able to do everything you need. All is required of you is to say "In Jesus Name or thank you Jesus for whatever the Holy Spirit of God have done on your behalf in order to complete the process because that's what my Father want and have said to do. This is another good reason why God is God. It is impossible for you to box Him in and say this is the only way he is going to operate. He can do things anyway He chooses. But as people, do we have any idea of what we are missing out on for not following the instructions God give us to use concerning the Holy Spirit of God? That's something to think about when you make time to do so.

64. Check Point # 16 and 17

Check Point # 16 .... Because you cannot see him, feel him, talk to him, since him, touch him, or hear him, doesn't mean he's not with you. To get to know Him or use His power, you have to follow God instructions. The Holy Spirit of God is always willing and ready for you. If you don't know He's with you and how to sense His presence, get help in that area of your life. To keep this simple, check with your pastors and men and women of God for instructions.

Check Point # 17 .... Can you name one positive thing that the devil has done for you? Can you name one thing that the devil have ever made or created? Can you name anything that you can think of that the devil has done for you or on your behalf? Note: Just because you cannot feel him, see him, sense him, hear him, touch him, or smell him doesn't mean he is not around. God have told us in His Word that the devil is going to and fro about the earth looking for trouble and destroying people and things. So let's keep it simple at this point and stay smart. Why would you want to follow the devil, in your mind, body, or spirit when he have never made or created anything, or have done anything good for anybody including the world. His job description is negative in every form you can imagine. His job among other things is to steal, kill, destroy, lie, cheat, cause problems, stress, turn people against God then destroys them and etc. Can you give me one positive reason why you will want to follow this guy? Choose to learn about God and His job description for the success of your life. Trust me, you can't go wrong with God.

THINK FOR REAL ....

Check Point # 18 ……………………….. (T-TRACOC-
FYU) = Things To Remember And Consider Or Claim For
Your Use.

T-Tracoc-Fyu # 1 ………………….. God will always
honor your faithful sincere heart. You must always remember
that God give you common sense that will assist you in
obeying the laws of the land at all times. When there is a
problem, seek counsel to acquire which laws will work in your
favor and take action on it. Never go to court without one of
your facts or proofs present with you. Everything must be with
you. Never lie to the judge because they have heard over a
thousand cases just like yours. If your untrue statement that
you are planning to use sounds good to you, that doesn't mean
it lines up with the law. Don't say it before the judge because
if he or she catches you in a lie it will be very difficult for you
after that to be counted as truthful or having clean hands in his
or her court. You do not go to court to ask question but rather
to state your claim. Ask your questions and get your answers
if any before you go to court. If you are not ready or need
more time, ask for it before you go to court. The way you
think at home or among your friends is different from the laws
of the land. On another point, a law can sound as if it belongs
to and applies to everyone. Always make sure that a law
specifically applies to you and your problem at hand. Every
law must in most cases have a Legislative Implementing
Regulation that will point you in the right direction of knowing if the law you are faced with applies to you and your case.
Without checking this, every law will sound as if it applies to
you and your case. Ignorance of the law is no excuse. The
bible also states that for the lake of knowledge my people
suffer and even perish. If you are a Christian, stay smart, do

your homework before you get out there. Always make checks and balances before you take any action. Make sure you have all your facts and proofs handy. Use your common sense and stay smart. Be of good report.

66. T-Tracoc-Fyu # 2 and 3

T-Tracoc-Fyu # 2 .... If you minister to someone or yourself for any reason and see no instant results; don't get discouraged because you try everything and nothing seems to work. Remember that God is Sovereign and regardless of all the things you do, God can still do it His way. But what is most important to remember is that from the time you started ministering to someone or yourself, the power of the Holy Spirit of God has already gone in and is at work on your behalf. Don't lose your healing at this point by undoing everything you have positively and correctly done. Stay smart, thank the Holy Spirit of God for completing the task in Jesus Name. Never get tire of thanking Him. Remember that thanking Him is far different from asking him. You are at the thanking Him point and stage, not at the asking Him point. Stay smart and claim your positive results.

T-Tracoc-Fyu # 3 .... Christianity is a way of life. It is saying and doing the same things Jesus did and walking in the same steps Jesus did, including men and women of God who spent their whole lives teaching, training, and showing us the ways of a Christian life style. Stay smart and put it to use.

67. T-Tracoc-Fyu # 4 and 5

T-Tracoc-Fyu # 4 .... (Daily Saying; Use this for such purpose). This day for me is the hour of power and action. I No longer will be willing to act or be a useless, weak, and spineless believer without power and miracles. I am a Christian. Christianity is a way of life. I chose to live this life style. I understand with my heart and not with my mind that because of the Holy Spirit of God living inside of me, I also have Jesus, and God the Father actually living inside of me from the top of my head to the bottom of my feet wanting to manifest themselves to the world in and through me. I thank you Jesus for the Holy Spirit of God that you have sent to me so I will be able to get the job done as the opportunity arises. I believe the Word of God is true and applicable in today's way of living. Thank you Holy Spirit of God in Jesus Name for your power in me that gets the job done as you live in me and teaches me all truths.

T-Tracoc-Fyu # 5 .... Philippians 2:13, For God who works in you to will and to act according to his good purpose. "I thank you Holy Spirit of God for Philippians 2:13 in Jesus Name that God is at work within me, helping me want to obey Him and then helping me do what He wants. This is good news".

68. T-Tracoc-Fyu # 6 and 7

T-Tracoc-Fyu # 6 .... Whenever it is your opportunity to cast out an evil spirit, you may want to start out by saying, "devil (or Satan) right now I bind you in the Name of Jesus and by the power of the Holy Spirit of God. In Jesus Name you foul spirit of (??) come out right now in the Name of Jesus". (Add at this point whatever you want or as your case may be) and end by saying; Thank you Jesus for doing it. Or you may say, thank you Holy Spirit of God for doing it in Jesus Name.

T-Tracoc-Fyu # 7 .... The Name of Jesus is above every other name. You cannot repeat this too much or say it too often. Every part of us belongs to Him. This is the best opportunity ever for you to receive Jesus as your Lord and Savior and thank Him for living in you. You may use this as a guide line when ministering salvation prayer to anyone. "Father, in the Name of Jesus, I ask you and thank you for forgiving me of all of my sins as I forgive those that have sinned against me. Jesus, I thank you for coming into my heart and living in me right now. I thank you that all my sins are forgiving and that I am born again this day. I am glad about it and I am happy that I am saved this day. I am a believer from this day forward in Jesus Name". Thank you Jesus for receiving me as your own. I am yours.

69. T-Tracoc-Fyu # 8

T-Tracoc-Fyu # 8 .... Stay smart, use common sense and make more positive choices each day than negative ones. It will be a pity if I was to inherit several Billion dollars and I'm not a Billionaire. It would also be pitiful if my funds grew and I didn't grow with it. Unless I can see a change in how I am, I will always have what I've got. But with focus, making more positive choices than negative ones in each given day, and persistence, I can have more than I've got today, because I can become more in my future than I am at this time in my life. If I share any good truths about Jesus Christ long enough, it will eventually enter the hearts of good people who are willing to accept the challenge to be something more than just average. Nothing is impossible with Jesus on my side. Together, we are unbeatable at any level. I really like it this way. I am glad about it. I am happy to continue in the Lord.

70. T-Tracoc-Fyu # 9

T-Tracoc-Fyu # 9 .... I thank you Holy Spirit of God for giving me seeds to plant so I will reap good results. I thank you for wisdom, knowledge, and understanding that you have given to me for my use. I thank you that I know who I am, what I want, and for the desires in my heart to line up with your Will for my life. I thank you for assisting me in gaining my success in every area of my life. I thank you Lord Jesus that your Word says if I seek or search, I will find. I thank you for giving me favor with God and men to pursue my desires with urgency before they loses their values and usefulness to me. I thank you also Holy Spirit of God for teaching me all truths which are just the start of my wealth gaining, learning, and positioning myself for success and learning to take action on your Word by faith. Thank you that this action also spiritually begins my miracle process of success in every area of my life. As I apply your training and teachings by faith in my life daily, I thank you for positive results in everything that concerns me. I thank you Lord Jesus that I am successful and my preparation on purpose lines me up for claiming my promises and blessings from you according to your Word for my life. I am happy with what I have in You Lord as I pursue all that I desire. I thank You Holy Spirit of God for dispatching my angel and assisting me with everything I have stated here that I have claimed as my. I thank you Jesus for making everything come to pass in this life time of mine in your precious Name. Thank you Jesus.

T-Tracoc-Fyu # 10 .... Assisting a suicide individual ...... Tell (him or her) that God loves (him or her), and want (him or her) to be free from this spirit of suicide if (he or she) will say Jesus, I thank you for forgiving me for my sins right now. I forgive anyone who has sinned against me. I even forgive myself for all my wrong thinking. I thank you also for coming into my heart right now. (At this point just look directly into the eyes of this individual, be firm, but with a soft voice – at medium level with authority and power, and cast out the evil spirit by saying something like this): "devil, I bind you in the Name of Jesus and by the power of the Holy Spirit of God, and I command you foul spirit of suicide to come out of (him or her) right now in Jesus Name. Thank you Jesus for doing it". (At this point, minister salvation and the baptism with the Holy Spirit to give (him or her) power to live successfully).

T-Tracoc-Fyu # 11 .... What to look for or inquire about when ministering to anyone with an illness or problem or symptoms............................... This general idea will assist you in what to ask about or what to look for. Use this as a starting point in finding a solution to the task at hand. Allow the Holy Spirit of God to guide you and direct you in gaining positive results. Remember that God is God and He can do things any way He wants to. So knowing all this, start of by:

A. Finding out what the problem is.

B. Address the problem itself and not the symptoms.

C. Listen carefully to what the individual is telling you about (his or her) problem.

D. Be practical in ministering healing to the specific problem.

E. Remember that nothing is impossible or difficult for God and you when you are using God's power to do all healings, so whatever (he or she) says the problem is; your response should be: "that's easy for God". I'm going to do my part right now in Jesus Name.

F. After you have ministered healing to (him or her), have (him or her) right then and there, put (his or her) faith into action by doing what (he or she) could not do before or by moving the problem area that could not move before. Continue to thank Jesus for your healing.

G. It is very important for (he or she) to say with (his or her) mouth, the words; "I thank you Jesus for my healing", because, this is what God commanded we do after the Holy Spirit of God have done the work. This is done in order to complete the healing. Never leave this out.

Edwin J. Dunbar Jr.

H.   There is so much more to learn and know about ministering to almost anything you come across but this is just a general idea to follow. Remember that from the start of your ministering, the power of the Holy Spirit of God is gone in and is at work so, don't let anyone lose their healing because they did not see an instant healing. Remind them to put their faith into action and continue to thank Jesus for their healing. You cannot do that with your mouth closed. Your ears have to hear what your mouth is saying. Be smart and reap your positive results.

73. T-Trcoc-Fyu # 12

T-Tracoc-Fyu # 12 .... Healing of memories (inner healing) such as: cruel treatment, insults, hurts, abuse, and many more usually caused by another person. You may say something like this: "Holy Spirit of God, I thank you right now in Jesus Name for taking your divine Spiritual eraser and removing all hurts of the past from this individual. I speak the peace of God upon (his or her) life in Jesus Name". (At this point, ask the individual to repeat after you): Start like this, "Lord Jesus, I forgive anyone who has hurt me and I thank you Lord for forgiving me for anyone that I've hurt". (Lay your hand on {his or her} head lightly and say; Jesus, I thank you right now for blessing this individual). Note: Make sure that someone is standing directly behind the individual and not touching (him or her). If (he or she) falls under the power of the Holy Spirit of God, catch (him or her) and lay (him or her) down softly and leave (him or her) there for the Holy Spirit of God to continue and finish his work. Assist (him or her) up when (he or she) is ready to get up. Check the results after (he or she) gets up.

T-Tracoc-Fyu # 13 .... Christianity is not a religion. It is a way of life that we live every day of our lives. Being Christ Like is a life style we enjoy 24 hours of every day we get to live. It is best to be and remain a man or a woman of God if you are a Christian. Remember always that Christ in you is your only hope of glory. Practice believing that He is actually living inside of you and anytime you stretch your hand towards someone while ministering to them, it is the hand of Jesus working through you and the power of the Holy Spirit of God being laid on the sick for their healing. The more this becomes a living reality in your life, the more you will be able to accomplish for the Kingdom of God where ever you live and speaking in any language you choose. Start believing today. Stay smart. Keep it simple.

75. T-Tracoc-Fyu # 14

T-Tracoc-Fyu # 14 …………….. Remember that the Name of Jesus is above every other name. You cannot repeat the name of Jesus too much or too often. The more you repeat the Name of Jesus, the better it is for you. Because of Jesus and the power of the Holy Spirit of God we have power and authority over the devil and to cast him out of people and to minister healing to all that desires it. Whenever you speak in the Name of Jesus or in Jesus Name, it means you are ministering by the authority Jesus has given to you as a believer. The choice is up to you to do or not to do. You will never be forced to act or to take action.

T-Tracoc-Fyu # 15 .... Understand that God's Word can never be limited to our human understanding. Note also that prayer or praying is different from commanding. You can't pray for everything. Some things must be commanded. Prayer generally is asking God for something or to do something. Commanding generally is to direct with authority, give orders to, and have control, or authority over the problem you are ministering to. Always do what God leads you to do because God doesn't always do things the way we think it should be done. Never forget that God is Sovereign. God is no respecter of persons. He doesn't care who you are or claim to be. So don't even think about using your man made title to impress Him. Don't waste your time and His. He just cares whether or not you are available and willing to do what he tells you to do. There is no neutral in faith. It is not a stationary thing or something that is standing in one spot or still. You can't put your faith in your pocket or prayer closet and take it out anytime you need to use it. Faith is something you must put into action now. Faith is what makes God move on your behalf. Be very natural. Be natural in whatever you do. If it doesn't sound like you, act like you, walk like you, talk like you, or look like you, make sure you check things out before you continue. Start by getting rid of "Self", so that you won't worry about what people think about you. You can't please everyone. For people who are against you or setting a trap for you, or wanting to interview you, beware, it is easier to say I am not qualify under your standard of doing business than to hank yourself in their traps. You are welcome to interview with me when you line up with God's standards according to the Word of God that I practice. This might not make them go away but will buy you some time to make checks and balances. The Holy Spirit of God will assist you if you let him work in and through you. Remember also when commanding or praying for someone, it is necessary for (he or she) to keep their big mouth shut. No one can transmit and receive at the same time. When you are praying for an individual and (he or she) is at the same time praying or talking while you are praying on their behalf, who is doing the listening? How can you all possibly be in agreement on anything when (he or she) doesn't have any idea or even know or for that matter hear what you are saying on (his or her) behalf? Make sure (he or she) keep that big mouth shut even if you have to place your finger lightly over it. Stay smart. Use your commonsense because you have one and enjoy the positive results that await you after you take action.

THINK FOR REAL ....

77. Check Point # 19

Check Point # 19 .... What should I do after I've blaspheme against the Holy Spirit of God?

1. God is God at all times. He means every word of what he said on the subject. He said and made all his rules at the beginning when he made man. He is the same yesterday, today, or tomorrow. He is not making up his rules as things come up. He said it once and even planted them in the hearts of men and women and for him that's enough.

2. If you are still alive after you commit this crime/sin, quickly repent and fast for a couple of days. I personally don't think that any human being can really do much for you at this point. And if they could, we would not be able to know the outcome or results of their efforts.

3. Clear the gap and speak to God. I believe that you and God can work this out. (A)   You are still alive and God have not allowed the devil to take your live. (B)   No one will know what took place between you and God. If you are still around and alive, well, and going strong, all people can say is that; "God is Sovereign" and only him alone can make any changes in what he says or does. No human being can judge God because we are not a God and cannot think or function at that level like God. This is another reason why the Holy Spirit of God is so important to us. You can call on Him and say Holy Spirit of God I messed up. Please forgive me and help me in Jesus Name. I thank you for forgiving me for what I've done. I repent right now in Jesus Name.

4. Walk a straight path with God after you repent. If God use you there after for anything he wants you to do, by all means do it. But make sure you are hearing from God and not the devil by checking the Word of God (The Bible). Only God can now turn your situation around. No man can. If I were in

your situation, I would continue serving God for as long as I can still breathe and have no stress about what God decide to do with me.

5.   Don't let the enemy of God, the devil, who is also our enemy as human beings get a hold of you. You can be sure that he is before God saying; he's mine, give him to me to do with as I please. Now we as human beings will never know what God and the devil talked about concerning you but if we see you doing well in the Lord and following His commands, our human thinking can only show us that we see everything according to our understanding which seems to be okay. But the truth of the matter is, this situation is strictly between you and God. In your thinking remember that nothing is impossible for God. Keep your eyes on Him. Don't give the devil one inch of lead way to get a hold of you. Keep it that way to the end of your existence on the earth. We will all learn from what we see and understand. The only thing we will be left with is: "did you go to Heaven or hell"? The good news is; this will be strictly between you and God. No man is going to assume or to be able to tell you that you are going to Heaven or hell. That's strictly between you and God. When we come to Heaven and see you there, we will then know that you made it. Likewise when we go to hell and see you there, we will then know that you didn't make it to Heaven. Stay smart and be of good report. Keep it simple. Choose Heaven.

THINK FOR REAL ....

78. Check Point # 20

Check Point # 20 ....

Keeping things simple ....

Luke 11:28,   Blessed rather are those who hear the Word of God and obey it.

Luke 12:23,   Life is more than food, and the body more than clothes.

Luke 12:25,   Who of you by worrying can add a single hour to his life?

Luke 12:34,   For where your treasure is, there your heart will be also.

Luke 16:10-13,   Whoever can be trusted with very little can also be trusted with much, and whoever is dishonest with very little will also be dishonest with much. So if you have not been trustworthy in handling worldly wealth, who will trust you with true riches? And if you have not been trustworthy with someone else's property, who will give you property of your own? No servant can serve two masters. Either he will hate the one and love the other, or he will be devoted to the one and despise the other. You cannot serve both God and money. (Note that it says serve and not spent. You can spent money wish is okay but you can't worship = serve it. You can worship God only and serve Him).

Luke 15:15,   You are the ones who justify yourselves in the eyes of men, but God knows your hearts. What is highly valued among men is detestable in God's sight.

Luke 17:3,   If your brother sins, rebuke him, and if he repents, forgive him.

Luke 17:6,   If you have faith as small as mustard seed, you can say to this mulberry tree, be uprooted and planted in the sea, and it will obey you.

Luke 17:20,   Once, having been asked by the Pharisees when the Kingdom of God would come, Jesus replied, "The Kingdom of God does not come with your careful observations nor will people say, here it is, or there it is, because the Kingdom of God is within you' or (among you).

Luke 21:14,   But make up your mind not to worry beforehand how you will defend yourselves.

Luke 22:67-70,   If you are the Christ or (messiah), they said, tell us. Jesus answered, If I tell you, you will not believe me, and if I ask you, you would not answer. But from now on, the son of man will be seated at the right hand of the mighty God. They all asked, are you then the son of God? "He replied, you are right in saying I am".

Luke 24:44-47,   He said to them, "This is what I told you while I was still with you: Everything must be fulfilled that is written about me in the Law of Moses, the prophets and the psalms". Then he opened their minds so they could understand the scriptures. He told them "this is written: The Christ will suffer and rise from the dead on the third day, and repentance and forgiveness of sins will be preached in his name to all nations, beginning at Jerusalem.

Proverb 18:21,   The tongue has the power of life and death, and those who love it will eat its fruit.

Proverb 28:9,   If anyone turns a deaf ear to the law, even his prayers are detestable.

Proverb 28:20,   A faithful man will be richly blessed but one eager to get rich will not go unpunished.

Proverb 28:22 & 25,   A stringy man is eager to get rich and is unaware that poverty awaits him. Likewise, "a greedy man stirs up dissension, but he who trust in the Lord will prosper".

John 15:7-19, if you remain in me and my words remain in you, ask whatever you wish and it will be given you. This is to my Father's glory, that you bear much fruit, showing yourselves to be my disciples. As the Father has loved me, so have I loved you. Now remain in my love. If you obey my commands, you will remain in my love, just as I obey my Father's commands and remain in His love. I have told you this so that my joy may be in you and that your joy may be complete. My command is this: love each other as I have loved you. Greater love has no one than this that He lay down His life for his friends. You are my friends if you do what I command. I no longer call you servants, because a servant does not know his master's business. Instead, I have called you friends, for everything that I learned from my Father I have made known to you. You did not choose me, but I chose you and appointed you to go and bear fruit – fruit that will last. Then the Father will give you whatever you ask in my Name. This is my command: Love each other. If the world hates you keep in mind that it hated me first. If you belonged to the world, it would love you as its own. As it is, you do not belong to the world, but I have chosen you out of the world.

Mark 9:38-41, "Teacher", said john, "we saw a man driving out demons in your Name and we told him to stop, because he was not one of us". Do not stop him, Jesus said. No one who does a miracle in my Name can in the next moment say anything bad about me, for whoever is not against us is for us. I tell you the truth, anyone who gives you a cup of water in my Name because you belong to Christ will certainly not lose his reward.

Mark 7:5-9 So the Pharisees and teachers of the law asked Jesus, "Why don't your disciples live according to the tradition of the elders instead of eating their food with unclean hands"? He replied, Isaiah was right when he prophesied about you hypocrites; as it is written: "The people honor me with their lips, but their hearts are far from me. They worship me in vain; their teachings are but rules taught by men. You have let go of the commands of God and are holding on to the traditions of men". And He said to them; you have a fine way of setting aside the commands of God in order to observe your own traditions.

Mark 1:23-28,   Just then a man in their synagogue who was possessed by an evil spirit cried out, what do you want with us Jesus of Nazareth? Have you come to destroy us? I know who you are – "The Holy One of God"! Be quiet! Said Jesus sternly. "Come out of him"! The evil spirit shook the man violently and came out of him with a shriek. The people were all so amazed that they asked each other, what is this? A new teaching – and with authority! He even gives orders to evil spirits and they obey Him. News about him spread quickly over the whole region of Galilee.

79. Check Point # 21

Check Point # 21 ………………….. Remember that the evil spirits and the Holy Spirit of God cannot share the same space. The power of the Holy Spirit of God is too strong for them and they will do whatever they need to do to get away. But here is the important part, do you have the Holy Spirit of God working in and through you or is He in you but you have no idea how to use His power within you?

THINK FOR REAL …………

80. Keeping Things Simple

Keeping Things Simple .... Matthews 28:17-20,   When they saw Him, they worshiped Him; but some doubted. Then Jesus came to them and said, "all authority in Heaven and on Earth has been given to me. Therefore go and make disciples of all nations, baptizing them in the Name of the Father and of the Son and of the Holy Spirit, and teaching them to obey everything I have commanded you. And surely I am with you always, to the very end of the age.

Matthews 18:18,   I tell you the truth, whatever you bind on earth will be bound in Heaven, and whatever you loose on earth will be loosed in Heaven.

Matthews 13:19 & 23,   When anyone hear the message about the Kingdom and does not understand it, the evil one comes and snatches away what was sown in his heart. But the one who received the seed that fell on good soil is the man who hears the Word and understands it. He produces a crop, yielding a hundred, sixty or thirty times what was sown.

Proverbs 19:5,9,11, & 20,   A false witness will not go unpunished, and he who pours out lies will not go free. A false witness will not go unpunished, and he who pours out lies will perish. A man's wisdom gives him patience; it is to his glory to overlook an offense. Listen to advice and accept instruction, and in the end you will be wise.

Proverbs 13:20,18,7,3, & 15,   He who walks with the wise grows wise, but a companion of fools suffers harm. He who ignores discipline comes to poverty and shame, but whoever heeds correction is honored. One man pretends to be rich, yet has nothing; another pretends to be poor, yet has great wealth. He who guards his lips guards his life, but he who speaks rashly will come to ruin. Good understanding wins favor, but the way of the unfaithful is hard.

Proverbs 12:26 & 1,   A righteous man is cautious in friendship, but the way of the wicked leads them astray. Whoever loves discipline loves knowledge, but he who hates corrections is stupid.

Proverbs 11:25,   A generous man will prosper; he who refreshes others will himself be refreshed.

81. Example # 5

Example # 5 .... Ministering to prostate problems including prostate cancer.

It is best to minister to the individual where you will be able to lay your hands on (him or her). For this example, you will have to lay hands on yourself and any affected areas. The first thing you should do is clear the gap. Next, you can do as follows: In the Name of Jesus, devil I bind you by the Holy Spirit of God's power and right now I break your power and cut off everything you have done to and in my body. I cast you out and command the prostate glands to shrink to normal size in Jesus Name. I command any and all roots of prostate problems or prostate cancer to die and come out right now in Jesus Name. I thank you Holy Spirit of God right now in Jesus Name for putting in my body a completely new and healthy system with everything working and functioning properly. I command a stress free and a relaxed functioning of all nerves, muscles, tendons, vertebrae, and ligaments and for the blood to work and function normally as the bone marrow produce healthy blood flows. (At this point you can lay your hands on or over the affected area if possible). I command every affected area of cancer cells from the roots to die and spread no more and come out in Jesus Name. I command the body's defensive "killer" cells to multiply and attack all prostate cancer cells if any is left in my body. I also command healing to all organs, scar tissues, and tissues affected and complete restoration of all parts where necessary. I rebuke all pain and command you brain to signal every area of my body for perfect functioning in Jesus Name. I thank you Holy Spirit of God for a creative miracle of a brand new immune system in my body right now in Jesus Name. Body you accept this system and brain you signal every part of my body for proper and normal operation and function in Jesus Name. Thank you Jesus for my healing. (Remember that God can do it any way He want to. He does not have to do what you have said here. But you have put your faith in action which is what makes God move on your behalf. You have done your part and I can guarantee you that God will never, never, never, let you get the upper hand on Him. He will look over His Word and perform it for you and nothing will return void or null. You will never win God. He will never fail to do His part because that's part of His job function and he just can't wait to give you what you have commanded. So don't even think about it. God wins every time. The glory always goes to God. You only get to keep the benefits. You do your part and He does His part.

THINK FOR REAL ....

Keep it simple ....

82. Check Point # 22

Check Point # 22 .... I want to be endued with the power of the Holy Spirit of God.

Well, this is an area where most people get stuck because of the lack of knowledge and unwillingness to face the facts and keep things simple. Before we go into details, let's look at this example: You see some cookies in a glass jar and you want those cookies. Do you want to get it out to talk to it or to eat it? It is very easy and simple to turn the cap or top, take it off and put your hand in this jar. However, for child safety reasons, the company had to change the easy top and put a different top that you now have to push down on and turn in order to get the cookies. Now your underage child can look at that cookie through the glass and turn the top but can't get those cookies because they don't have the strength needed to push down on the top and then turn it to open the jar. Without instructions and the needed strength, they will turn and turn and turn that top thinking they can get in but getting nowhere or no positive results and no closer to eating those cookies. This will make them angry, causing a lot of noise until some-one of age and strength comes and assists the little ones and give them some cookies. After they eat the cookies given to them, they will be ready for more and they will look at that jar and once again try to get it open because they can see those cookies and the cookies are saying to them; I know you can see me, I taste real good, you are welcome to eat me if you can open this jar. Now these little ones make a few more turns and nothing happens for them. They make a little bit of fuss and noise but this time they quickly remembered who opened that jar for them to get some cookies. So now they use their common sense and take that jar to the same person to open it or an adult to open that jar because they can still see those cookies looking at them saying you can eat me if you can get me out of this jar. If they don't know how to get that cookie out of that jar, the cookie will always be there uneaten until they learn how to push down and turn the cap or top to open the jar. So it is with the Holy Spirit of God's power. You want and need the Holy Spirit power. You ask him to come in and live in you. He did and is very happy you asked Him to. But you still have to learn how to use that power he has. He want you to use it because that's part of His reasons for being here on earth but you can't because you don't know how to open that jar and start putting that power to use. He said I have made everything simple and easy for you to make use of this power. I am here, says the Holy Spirit of God for you anytime and anyplace you need me. So now you know it is not enough for you to just ask Him to come and live in you. He wants you to use Him to continue the work of God on the earth. But with no training and knowledge of how to get your hands on that power which is greatly needed, the devil will come to you and say; "You don't really need that power. You can call on Jesus but it is not necessary to disturb Jesus because no one is after you". Positively, we are so blessed that Jesus never says to us why are you messing with me when I've already given you the Holy Spirit to take care of everything that concerns you. The devil will also tell you that you have nothing to worry about and it is enough just for you to be saved in order to make it in to Heaven. Next, if anybody calls you a weak and spineless Christian it is because they are not going to make it to Heaven and is trying to take you to hell with them. Don't listen to them, God is very big and everything is difficult and takes a lot of time and years to get close enough to finding out what to do says the devil. (Note in this sentence how the words are twisted to confuse the everyday individual). But the Holy Spirit of God is in you at this time saying to you don't listen to this guy he is the devil and he's telling you all the wrong things. But you grieve the Holy Spirit of God and can't even hear Him when He talks to you. Now, remember, that just because you can't see the devil, feel him, smell him, taste him, touch him, or hear him doesn't mean he is not around you at all times. When you have things that God have given you to use that are very simple to use and they become difficult and confusing which 99 % of it takes place in your mind, you can safely note that the devil is messing with you. The other 1 % is strictly you where you have chosen not to follow the ways of God and the will He has for your life with the Holy Spirit of God. Now we still want to get to use the power that is within us. So let's understand that we are the jar. The Holy Spirit of God lives inside of us. He is doing us no good just by living inside of us. We need to know how to open the jar so we can have access to this power that Jesus sent back to earth to live in us and do everything for us. First, let's list some important things here: Keeping it simple..........

A. The Holy Spirit is the go to guy who takes care of everything for you. You do your part first then He does his part.

B. After He does His part, our part is to complete this process by saying "In Jesus Name" or "thank You Jesus".

C. The Holy Spirit is in charge of our angel that was created for us. We as human beings cannot give them instructions on our behalf. If we don't know about them we can't use them on our behalf.

D. The Holy Spirit is the Chief. He does not get his hands dirty. He is the One that dispatches your angel and or the angel of the Lord on your behalf.

E. The Holy Spirit of God is the One who monitors the earth, teaches you all truths, show you all hidden riches, give you the needed power to accomplish everything God has lined up for your life here on earth, and etc.

F. The Holy Spirit of God is the One who have everything that we need for our success here on the earth. Why will you let Him live inside of you and not try to get your hands on all that power and everything God has for you and your future?

G. The knowledge and wisdom that the Holy Spirit has for you is excellent and unmatched with anything you compare it with. He's the One who makes your Bible come alive to you and renews your mind. When you speak in tongues you also edify yourself. He also takes what you are saying to God and makes it your perfect prayer to God.

H. If you have not receive the Holy Spirit of God and His power, do it now and for those who have received Him but have no knowledge of how to use Him, keep it simple by asking Jesus right now to baptize you with the Holy Spirit. Lift your hands up to God with no frowning but with a smile and begin to praise Him, but not in any language that you know. (Remember to keep it simple. Use e-te-be-te Little syllables) and start expressing sounds of love so the Holy Spirit can take whatever sounds you make or give Him, and make it for you, the perfect prayer Language that only Him, God, and Jesus can understand wish will turn any ordinary individual into an extraordinary person. Let your spirit soar as it talks to God for the very first time. You can make sounds of praises to Him using your e-te-be-te little syllables singing to Him your love song. You can use your e-te-be-te little syllables to speak to Him slowly or rapidly. You can start and stop anytime you choose to. Remember that God reserved this unknown Language to man for Him alone. When you speak it or sing it, it is from you directly to God. The Holy Spirit of God takes it and makes it exactly what you should be saying to God. The devil understands every Language on the earth except this one. Being that you don't understand what you are speaking or singing to God, the devil can't understand it as well. This makes the devil very angry, because there is nothing on the earth that he doesn't know about. He is not about to let you get away with that. The devil will now come at you with his first attack on your mind by saying, that can't be right. Anything of this nature is of the devil. You can't say that because it is not spiritual. You are making the sounds and there is no God in it only you. Listen to yourself, you sound crazy and stupid. Everyone will laugh at you because you are unreal and sounds useless and sorry full. After the devil have run this on your mind, don't listen to your mind or others of ignorance on these negative sayings because if you were standing among some friends and a few of them moved over to the side to talk about you and a few others there, you would be saying the same things similar to what the devil will be saying to you or in your mind. Because you want to know what they are saying but you can't hear them and you are not close enough to ease drop = trying to hear on the sly what they are saying and about who. Now it is entirely up to you whether you open that jar and get the Holy Spirit of God and everything He has to offer you.

1 Corinthians 14:2-3, For anyone who speaks in a tongue (or another language unknown to men) does not speak to men but to God. Indeed, no one understands him; he utters mysteries with his spirit (or by his spirit). But everyone who prophesies speaks to men for their strengthening, encouragement and comfort.

Acts 1:8, You will receive power when the Holy Spirit comes on you. (Note: This doesn't mean you know how to open the jar and use that power).

83. Check Point # 23

Check Point # 23 ……………………… When you ask Jesus to baptize you with the Holy Spirit and you speak in tongue or a language unknown to man how do you know you really are? (I'm glad you asked).

A. You must make all the sounds with your own mouth and not in your mind. You must open your mouth and talk as if you were talking to somebody. You can't do it with your mouth closed.

B. Your ears must be able to hear your voice and know that it is really you making each sound.

C. You must open your mouth to make the sounds or pronounce the syllables. If you keep your mouth shut, you do nothing and you get nothing. No one is going to open your mouth for you, and the Holy Spirit is not going to open your mouth for you. Don't look for any kind of special or certain kind of feeling to open your mouth for you because it wouldn't work and might be from the enemy of God trying to pull a fast one to turn you away from this power. Always remember that you do your part than God does His part.

D. Any sounds coming from your nose because of your mouth being closed is null and void.

E. Any sounds forming in our mind and your mouth is not speaking it is null and void.

F. If you are making the sounds and it doesn't sound like you or your own voice, check yourself. Something is wrong. Make sure nothing spooky is going on.

G. If you are making your sounds or syllables and your ears cannot hear them, check your mouth. It might be closed. If it is closed, open it and continue making your sounds. Keep it simple. This doesn't mean that you find one word and repeat it over and over, or rapidly or slowly. A word, fast or slow is still the same word. If you can understand that word, it still will not qualify for an unknown language to men because the devil can also understand the word. The power is not in what you are saying. It's in what the Holy Spirit is doing with what you are saying. Your part is easy. The Holy Spirit of God does all the hard parts.

H. If you are looking for a certain or special feeling to prompt you to start and make your sounds, it is null and void. You don't look for a certain or special feeling to make you talk to anyone you chose to talk to. You just talk to people if you have something to say to them and make adjustments along the way. The same rules apply here. The only difference here is, you are not speaking in any language you know. Just a bunch of e-te-be-te little syllables put together coming from your mouth, using your voice and making the sounds. After some practice, just watch, listen, and hear how the Holy Spirit of God will give you a perfect language that will flow out of you like you knew what you were speaking. At this point you will enjoy it and feel good about yourself but you still will not know what you are saying. If you are or start speaking a language that you know, just stop and start over. Pay close attention from here on and see how your life will change for the better.

I. If you are speaking any language known on the earth or in the world, it is null and void.

J. If you are crying because you don't know what to do or you want to use that as your way of speaking or making your sounds, it is null and void. This is real life. Not a game.

K. When you are speaking and making your sounds and you can understand the words you are speaking, it is null and void.

L. Practice as much as you want every day until you develop a fluent language. Remember that the Holy Spirit of God always does the hard and difficult parts. All He requires of you is to put your faith into action = start first.

M. Now in keeping things simple let's look at the phase or statement, "put your faith into action". Let's break this down into easy and simple understanding. All this means is start first and don't stop until you have finished the task or whatever you are saying or doing. After you do this, Hebrews 11:1, will follow. "Now faith is being sure of what we hope for and certain of what we do not see", or "faith is the substance of things hoped for and the evidence of things not seen". Remember; you do your part first and then God does his part. Without you doing your part first, there is no faith in action present. So put everything aside, out of your way or thinking and out of your mind that would keep your mind occupy and just start first.

THINK FOR REAL ....

Check point # 24 .... Salvation .... Let's take a quick look at Salvation. What is important here?

1. Asking Jesus to forgive you for your sins and invite Him to come and live in and through you and be your Lord and Savior.

2. After you repent and turn away from those sins, put your faith into action by thanking Him for forgiving you for your wrong doings against others as you also forgive others for any wrong doings against you. It is equally important for you to forgive yourself and not hold on to any negative things. Note: Thanking Jesus for this is saying to Him, "I believe you have forgiven me and is now living in me. At this point you are also saying to Jesus; I have not seen any physical signs yet but I know you have given me what I have asked you for. I have no doubt that you have answered my request. This is faith in action on your part and Jesus will look over His Word to perform it for you.

3. Now that you are saved, your next step should be; asking Jesus to baptize you with the Holy Spirit. This will assist you in gaining everything God has for you while living the Christian life style. Read your Bible daily and ask the Holy Spirit to open the Word and let it come alive to you as you renew your mind daily.

4. Find a church if you don't already have one that you will like to attend. Stay there under the watchful eyes and teachings and training from your ministers and pastors. You cannot by-pass this part and do your own thing. This is where you will learn, grow, and live the Christian life style.

5. Always check with your pastors and ministers in matters of concern. Never take the law in your own hands by following others in your place of worship who are not in

agreement with your leaders. Some people feel that they know more than your leaders that God has placed over your church. Follow no one that God have not put in charge. Be smart and use your common sense because the devil goes to church also. His intentions are never good. But no need to worry. The difference between you, your ministers, and your pastors are; they have the power and knowledge to overcome and they will gain control. Learn, grow, and stay save. But never stop at salvation. There is much more to learn while living the Christian life style.

85. Conclusion

I thank you Jesus for forgiving me for my wrong doings as I forgive those who have wronged me. I thank you for this breakthrough to you. I thank you Father God for creating my angel that is assign to me and is in charge of me and my safety. I thank you Holy Spirit of God for living inside of me and dispatching my angel on my behalf. I thank You for completing me and making me the person you want me to be as I follow your instructions for my success. I thank you for opening my spiritual eyes, ears, mind, and heart so that I will gain the knowledge, wisdom, and understanding you have for me. I thank you for making everything that pertains to life and God's will for my success to come to pass in the natural for me as you also open my natural eyes, ears, mind, and heart for total balance in my Christian life style. I thank you for your power in me and the opportunity to serve you as my Lord and King. I thank you also for the message you placed on these pages for me to be blessed. As you renew my mind, I thank you for assisting me to put them to work for my success in doing your Will for my life. I thank you for baptizing me with the Holy Spirit and with all his power that he is teaching me how to use for the glory of God. I thank you that I am born again. I thank you for being a blessing to me and giving me an opportunity to live the Christian life style and to share with others you have sent my way or placed in my path. I love you Father and I thank you for loving me and looking over your Word to perform it for me daily in Jesus Name. A-men.

www.ingramcontent.com/pod-product-compliance
Lightning Source LLC
La Vergne TN
LVHW051628080426
835511LV00016B/2232